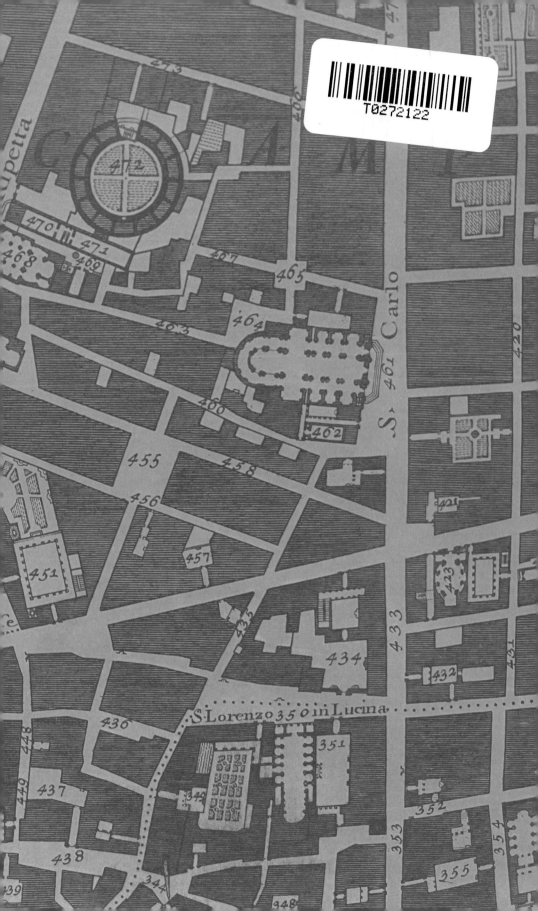

◆

AN ARCHITECT'S
ADDRESS BOOK

◆

ORO Editions
Publishers of Architecture, Art, and Design
Gordon Goff: Publisher

www.oroeditions.com
info@oroeditions.com

Published by ORO Editions

Copyright © Robert Lemon 2023
Text and Images © Robert Lemon 2023
All photos by author unless noted in Photo Credits

All rights reserved. No part of this book may be reproduced, stored in a retrieval system, or transmitted in any form or by any means, including electronic, mechanical, photocopying of microfilming, recording, or otherwise (except that copying permitted by Sections 107 and 108 of the U.S. Copyright Law and except by reviewers for the public press) without written permission from the publisher.

You must not circulate this book in any other binding or cover and you must impose this same condition on any acquirer.

SPONSORS
The Christopher Foundation
Vancouver Heritage Foundation
Yosef Wosk

Copy editor and indexer: Meridith Murray
ORO Managing Editor: Kirby Anderson

Cover and book design: Pablo Mandel / circularstudio.com
Typeset in Adobe Minion Pro

10 9 8 7 6 5 4 3 2 1 FIRST EDITION

Library of Congress data available upon request. World Rights: Available

ISBN: 978-1-954081-96-3

Color Separations and Printing: ORO Editions, Inc.
Printed in China.

International Distribution: www.oroeditions.com/distribution

ORO Editions makes a continuous effort to minimize the overall carbon footprint of its publications. As part of this goal, ORO Editions, in association with Global ReLeaf, arranges to plant trees to replace those used in the manufacturing of the paper produced for its books. Global ReLeaf is an international campaign run by American Forests, one of the world's oldest nonprofit conservation organizations. Global ReLeaf is American Forests' education and action program that helps individuals, organizations, agencies, and corporations improve the local and global environment by planting and caring for trees.

(◆ ◆ ◆)

AN ARCHITECT'S ADDRESS BOOK

the places that shaped a career

◆

ROBERT LEMON

◆

ORO Editions — Novato, California

CONTENTS

INTRODUCTION

"WHO WOULD WANT to read your memoir?" was the tart rejoinder from a friend, a writer whom I had asked for advice on how to write a book and get it published. She was probably right. I am not a titled architect like Lord Foster, nor am I a Nobel-winning writer like Alice Munro. The number of my Instagram followers is in the low three digits, so I am hardly an influencer. Advice noted, I forged ahead anyway, partly out of vanity, I suppose, but with a gut feeling that the circumstances and places that had shaped my life as an architect might just possibly be of interest to others.

People seem to be fascinated by architecture and what an architect does. I have been told wistfully by many friends and clients that they had always wanted to be an architect. Representing the overlap of art and science, architecture is often associated with some kind of alchemy combining creativity and good taste. The heroic figures of Howard Roark and Frank Lloyd Wright fuel that image. The flood of design and shelter media in recent years, from *HGTV* to *Dwell, Elle Decor* and the grande dame of design porn, *Architectural Digest*, have turned everyone into authorities on design. But what qualities actually make an architect? And why would I want to be one? And how does where you live influence one's career?

Address Book is more than a travel journal or little black book. My memoir is structured around the places and addresses where I have actually lived, usually long enough to have a mailing address. So this is not just a recollection of lovely places and interesting buildings. It's about settling into a place for a while, living there, making friends, researching and working, and definitely eating and drinking along the way; food features conspicuously in most of the chapters.

(•◆•)

I am a gay white male, hail from United Empire Loyalist stock and grew up in a small city in southwestern Ontario. I am named after my father, who was a civil engineer and land surveyor. My mother was a homemaker. I have an older brother and younger twin brothers, all of whom still live in Ontario.

After being rejected by two schools of architecture, I ended up receiving two prizes and graduating at the top of my class at Carleton's School of Architecture six years later. I have had study terms abroad in Paris and London, and I began my graduate degree in Rome, ending with an MA in conservation in York. I have lived in Vancouver since 1979, and for most of those years had a life partner, Bob Ledingham, an interior designer more celebrated than I. He died nine days shy of our thirty-two years together.

I have worked as an architect in private practice and also as a city hall bureaucrat. In the course of my career, I have written articles for professional journals, dry-as-toast city council reports and some more readable articles for shelter magazines. I have presented papers on Vancouver's modern architecture at conferences in Banff, Bratislava, Miami and Stockholm. I have also penned short tributes to friends and relatives who have died for the "Lives Lived" column of Toronto's *Globe and Mail*.

Within the rather narrow field of Canadian heritage conservation, I have received some modest recognition, for which I have a wall full of heritage awards. I have written or contributed to standards, guidelines and building codes for heritage buildings, and I have served on the boards of many heritage organizations. I am happy to support charities that encourage the arts, education and heritage conservation. My résumé fits crisply on one page, but my *curriculum vitae* expands to eleven (single-spaced) pages.

I enjoy travel, visiting historic and modern houses and gardens, opera, art and food. I am told that I am a good cook. Having shunned athletics in my youth, I discovered triathlons as well as skate-skiing in midlife. My career as an amateur athlete includes two half-Ironmans, many Olympic-distance triathlons, several long bike tours and five cross-country ski races in Idaho. I have competed in Gay or Out Games in Amsterdam, Sydney, Montreal and Copenhagen.

I now have a husband named Franco Monfort. He is Filipino, reasonably tall, very handsome and sometimes quite silly. He can carry on a conversation about French politics at a fancy dinner party with a Parisian.

And I am jealous of his splendid head of thick, jet-black hair. He loads the dishwasher better than I do. He patiently listens while I read draft chapters of *Address Book* to him. Otherwise, his red pen corrections would be scribbled all over the printed drafts.

(• ♦ •)

I believe that how you grow up, where you have lived and the people who influenced you along the way are all part this memoir. And having a curiosity for old buildings and their designers has shaped my interest in being an architect.

For example, Rome is my favourite city, and while architects over the centuries have been inspired by wandering the streets of the *centro storico*, I actually walked those streets every day for most of the six months I lived there. Twice a day I would pass the Pantheon going to and from my conservation studies at ICCROM, and it became familiar and part of my life there, not just a site to be seen. I charted my route on my copy of Giambattista Nolli's 1748 map of Rome. Very little has changed in the intervening 275 years.

Certainly, the architects I admire and mention in my stories – Alvar Aalto, Pierre Chareau, Norman Foster, Edwin Lutyens, Andrea Palladio, Carlo Scarpa and Robert Venturi – are well known. But the people whom I have met or who have influenced me over the years and who are not well known – Paul Baldwin, Agnès Cailliau, Penny Graham, Jean Hodgins, Jean Johnson, Bente Lange, Clark McDougall, Bill Reed, Meredith Sykes and Martin Weaver – deserve some recognition as well. My late partner Robert Ledingham deserves a prominent mention, perhaps a whole book. Most of the chapters focus on someone whom I respect and wish to thank for the influence they have had on me. And I think they deserve to be known and recognized for their contributions.

The chapters are organized in chronological order, except for the second-to-last. "Orchard Beach, Montezuma, Stratford" should have been placed earlier in the chronology, but the connections between my Aunt Jean's cottage and my new home at "seven&nine" placed it as the penultimate chapter. But I think you could jump in at any address that sounds interesting and get a picture of that place and its influence on me.

I must confess that a couple of the chapters do not exactly fit the criteria of my having a mailing address there. Much as I love Copenhagen, I have not actually resided on "Tordenskjoldgade" (and thus was spared having to spell it in the return address), but I have visited Bente Lange so often at her flat there, and she has been so helpful in my career, that I felt it belonged. Nor have I lived in Los Angeles (or would ever want to) but my work on a remarkable Moroccan house "Just off Melrose" justified its inclusion. "Wessex" is a similar story; it is a place I have visited many times but have never actually "lived". However, working on an eighteenth-century farmhouse there, even briefly, qualifies it for inclusion.

One more caveat: I am sad to say that the journals of the half year I spent in Rome and Italy in 1984, as recounted in "Largo di Fontanella di Borghese", were badly water damaged some time ago. The top quarter of each page has blurry ink smudges where there should be dates, places and details. But, as *Address Book* is a memoir, I can honestly say that it is "as I recall", if perhaps not exactly as experienced.

Lest you think I was name dropping at the outset of this introduction, I have never met Norman Foster but did have the pleasure of working with Foster+Partners on Jameson House in Vancouver. I would love to meet Alice Munro and thank her for "The Turkey Season" which I read in *The New Yorker* in 1980 when I was visiting my parents.

It reminds me of our shared Southwestern Ontario roots.

There is something about Alice's way with words that evokes the taciturn nature of the places she writes about, not far from where I grew up. And while I never worked gutting turkeys, as a teenager I sweated in the warehouse of the local Canadian Tire store for a summer, unloading greasy mufflers and exhaust pipes from trailer trucks, sweeping the floor with Dustbane, and punching a time clock. While trying to fit in with the coffee break chatter of my coworkers, I nonetheless always felt they wondered about my sexuality. Finally leaving St. Thomas to study architecture spared me from a life like that of the fictional Herb Abbott at the Turkey Barn in the real Logan, Ontario. I came out to my parents not long after reading Alice's story.

And so we begin.

(♦)

12 ROSEBERY PLACE

S HE SAT QUIETLY on the edge of the bed, looking out over the lawns of the nicer houses to the east as I applied the lipstick I had found hidden away at the bottom of her dresser drawer. On the day of my father's funeral, I was dressing my mother.

In my mother's closet was a black wool bouclé Chanel-style suit with handmade braided frog closures. The suit had been made for her decades ago, no doubt from a Simplicity pattern, by her mother, who was an excellent seamstress. By now, mom's own illnesses had withered her so much that the suit was much too large, but I had her try it on anyway. I bought a slip for her for the occasion, as she no longer had one.

Once I brushed her silver hair, put on a black headband and clasped her strand of cultured pearls around her neck, she looked beautiful again, much as she had when she, my father and my older brother moved into the house at 12 Rosebery Place St. Thomas, Ontario, in September 1954, just two weeks before I was born.

There is no doubt that growing up on a tree-lined street in a small city in southwestern Ontario with a rich history and a remarkable collection of historic buildings influenced my interest in architecture. Also influential was my family's history in the city and my aunt and uncle's rescuing of a landmark house. Important too was a particularly talented high school history teacher who shared with our class his fascination with and detailed research into the architectural history of Elgin County.

The houses my mother gazed upon that morning were much grander than ours, set back from the street with spacious front lawns on lots that stretched back to one of the deep ravines that cut through the city. The closest house belonged to the owners of the local Canadian Tire store, where all the Lemon boys had worked summer jobs. Their Colonial Revival house had southern plantation pretensions and a pool in the back-yard, where we were sometimes invited to swim.

The next house to the east was a large yellow brick Italianate Revival mansion, owned by a lawyer. It was situated at the foot of Hincks Street and had all the trappings of a grand Victorian home – centre hall plan, wrap-around porch, tall dark green shuttered windows and formal plantings.

Next door at number 24 was my favourite house on the street, the Anderson's handsome Georgian Revival. It was two storeys high with a steeply pitched hipped roof clad in gray slate shingles and sat formally on a raised parterre. I was fascinated by its exterior of dark purple vitrified bricks.[1] With its tight eaves – a term that I would later learn meant that it had no overhanging soffits – and a simple course of painted dentils and plain detailing, it had an elegant, rather chaste expression. It was rumoured to be a renovation of an older house, and I have recently learned that the original 1912 four-square simple Edwardian design with a broad front porch was radically renovated in 1952 to become the handsome Georgian Revival house it is now. My fascination with this house likely foretold my interest in architecture, and references to it pop up in many chapters of *Address Book*.

---

1 Vitrification is the result of firing bricks at a very high temperature and chemicals like magnesium create a dark purplish colour.

The front door had a special knob, placed in the centre of its raised panel, to complete the symmetry of the façade. I was intrigued by how the latch could work with the knob in the middle of the door. The same door-knob arrangement can be seen at No. 10 Downing Street, but there the door is opened for the prime minister from the inside. The circular drive-way sported a late model Jaguar XKE, confirming the family's prominence in town as owners of Anderson's Department Store on Talbot Street. Later, when the trees along the street had to be chopped down, the Andersons had Russian olive trees planted along the boulevard in front of their house, a decision that I thought was rather exotic for St. Thomas.

And then there was the Davidsons' Tudor Revival house, which was home to a future architect, closer to my older brother's age, who later became my first employer after graduation when I moved to Vancouver. Farther east was an enormous copper beech tree – one of the largest in Canada – which loomed over the front yard of another grand Victorian. After its stretch of five blocks, Rosebery Place ended at the grain silos along the London & Port Stanley railway tracks at Princess Street. The spires of Alma College, a noted private girl's school in an impressive Gothic Revival edifice not unlike the buildings of Parliament Hill, could be seen just across the tracks.[2]

(• ◆ •)

---

2 Many of St. Thomas's old buildings have been demolished, –including Alma College after a fire in 2008.

I am the middle child of four boys between my older brother Peter and younger twins David and Paul and am named after my father, perhaps because I resembled him as an infant and was called Rob by my family. My middle name comes from his brother, my uncle Gordon. My father, Robert Lloyd Lemon (Bob), was named after Robert Borden, the Canadian prime minister of the day, and David Lloyd George, his British counterpart. He was raised in a large redbrick Victorian house with a turret and a fancy fretwork porch at 100 Wellington Street, the youngest of four children of Frank Arden Lemon, a pharmacist (and alderman at one point) and his second wife, Blanche.

The building housing Lemon's Drug Store was located on Talbot Street, the two-mile-long main drag, at the corner of John Street. The bronze

letters L E M O N S are still there, embedded in the terrazzo sidewalk, but the building now houses a restaurant. I have in my possession a tiny glass measuring vial with the imprint "Lemon's Drug Store, 633 Talbot Street, phone 11", indicating it was one of the first places in town to have a telephone. The drug store featured a soda fountain, where my father worked making chocolate syrup for the malted milkshakes that remained a mainstay of his diet throughout his life. In our family, a chocolate malt was always made with Shaw's vanilla ice cream (not chocolate), chocolate syrup and Horlick's malt powder. After drug store soda fountains became a thing of the past, Dad brought home one of the mint-green Hamilton Beach milkshake makers, and he would regularly treat us to a malt.

During World War II, Dad served in the RAF as a navigator, training at nearby Fingal, then in Prince Edward Island, before heading overseas to Iceland, Ireland and England. He kept a photo of his air force buddies in his wallet. I suppose his wartime duty, while difficult, must have been an adventure. I am sure I inherited my interest in geography and travel, and my good sense of direction, from him.

After the war, my newly married parents lived in Toronto. Mom worked as a receptionist while Dad earned his bachelor of science degree in civil engineering at the University of Toronto. Education completed, they returned to St. Thomas to start their family. Dad also became an Ontario land surveyor.

I can recall visiting my father's office, with the drafting tables and a set of bronze French curve templates that he used to make drawings of culverts, drainage canals, road rights-of-way and parcel boundaries, measured in chains and furlongs and drawn in ink on "linens". The drawing material was actual linen cloth – chosen for its reliability to retain its scale – that had been coated with an emulsion to make it possible to draw on. This stability was also helpful for archival purposes, when the drawings were deposited in the Land Registry Office. I was fascinated one day when he took a small piece of this drawing material to the bathroom sink to dissolve the coating. White linen fabric appeared like magic. Not so magical was the smell of benzene, the chemical in the ancient blueprint machine next to his desk, which he used to make duplicate copies. Who knows what toll the benzene fumes took on my father's health? Dad developed diabetes and Alzheimer's disease in his later years.

Dad walked to work each day, up Hincks Street to his office at Bell Lemon and Houghton, Ontario Land Surveyors. He came home for lunch, as did all the boys, as our public school was just a block away. Lunch would often be Campbell's tomato soup and a grilled cheese sandwich, which my mother would make for the six of us. Or sometimes Lipton's chicken noodle soup from a packet. If we were lucky, she would have made macaroni and cheese, with large shreds of local aged white Mapleton cheddar, or at least the boxed Kraft Dinner version. I could eat an entire box of KD by myself.

Dad's work involved field visits for surveying and engineering projects across Elgin County, and he would often take the family with him on Sunday drives around the township roads and tobacco fields to check on his culverts. In the summertime, we would usually stop in Port Stanley to visit Dad's sister Jean at her cottage, where we would have a lunch of fried yellow perch on the screened porch, then an ice cream at Shaw's on the way home. Sometimes we would just take a rural drive, with a stop for a steamed hot dog at Mackie's on the boardwalk at the Port's Main Beach, where the orangeade has been famous since 1911. In the winter, we would drive to Port just to see how the cottage was weathering.

Norma Eileen, my mother, was the youngest of the Miller family's three girls. My grandfather, Harold, had been an engineer on the New York Central Railroad, commanding the diesel trains that travelled daily through southwestern Ontario. The straight line for American trains to connect Buffalo and Detroit happened to pass right through St. Thomas. That strategic location spurred a robust period in the city's history and played an important role in my family. St. Thomas is known as "The Railway City".

The Miller family lived up on Redan Street, not far from the Grand Trunk Railway line that was the site of the infamous death of Jumbo, the world's largest elephant, in 1885. After shows in St. Thomas, when Jumbo was being herded up into a Barnum and Bailey Circus boxcar, he was killed by another train. A concrete statue of *an* elephant now stands at the west entry to Talbot Street, marking the city's rather tragic claim to fame. Oddly, it is not even a replica, as it is bigger than Jumbo and has much nicer tusks. I suppose civic pride may have led to the enhancements. Jumbo's actual hide ended up at Tufts University, where P.T. Barnum was a trustee, until it was destroyed by a fire in 1974. The Tufts sports teams are still called "Jumbos". His skeleton (Jumbo's not Barnum's) is stored in the Brooklyn warehouse of the American Museum of Natural History.

"JUMBO"— Killed in St. Thomas, September 15, 1885   COMPLIMENTS OF ANDERSONS LIMITED. ST. THOMAS. ONT

Much smaller than my towering father, Mom was seriously outnumbered in her household of five men. At one point all four boys overlapped at high school, and she managed to send us off every morning, each of us with a freshly ironed shirt. Her escape was curling, a popular winter sport in southwestern Ontario. Born with different coloured eyes, one of them blind, she managed to be very skilled at the sport, something that requires good depth perception. In the 1960s, she travelled with her team from the St. Thomas Curling Club to bonspiels in nearby places like Tillsonburg, Ingersoll, Aylmer and Mount Pleasant. Her team usually won, but she rarely stayed to socialize at the club.

My parents smoked constantly – Macdonald Export "A" plain, no filters – but they did not drink at all, nor did they entertain except for family gatherings (my mother's two sisters lived just blocks away). For much of my childhood, mom's mother, my Nanny, would host all the big family dinners – Thanksgiving, birthdays and Christmas – and she would prepare everything from scratch. For my birthday, Nanny would make an entire lemon meringue pie just for me.

(•◆•)

St. Thomas is a small city of 40,000 people in the middle of Elgin County. Established in the first decade of the nineteenth century, it was the main town of Colonel Thomas Talbot's estate, a vast land reserve of five thousand acres along the north shore of Lake Erie, granted to him by Lieutenant Governor Simcoe in 1803. Talbot's development of the territory included laying out the Talbot Road, which extended for three hundred miles from Windsor to Lake Ontario. Today Ontario Highway 3 more or less follows the course of the old Talbot Road for the same length. Many of the early settlers were United Empire Loyalists, escaping the newly formed republic across the lake. They had to clear the dense Carolinian forest to create fields to grow the hemp and tobacco they planted. Later settlers were immigrants fleeing poverty and famine in Scotland and Ireland in the mid-nineteenth century.

It is widely held that Thomas Talbot named the town after himself, despite the fact that he was more of a despot than a saint. The picture-perfect Old St. Thomas' Church in Gothic Revival style dates from 1822, with a lych-gate and graveyard outside and box pews inside. It is one of the finest old churches in Ontario.

My aunt Kay has traced the Lemon family tree and found that there is a trail of Lemons who first arrived in Fort Erie, Upper Canada (now Ontario), in 1798 from Pennsylvania, although my brother argues that they were from Bucks County, not Lancaster County as I thought (I have been to Lancaster, the centre of Amish country, and can attest there are many pages of Lemons in the local phone book). Even earlier, there were Lemons in New Jersey and Massachusetts in the first part of the eighteenth century, but the trail peters out in Europe earlier than that. In French, Lake Geneva is Lac Leman, so perhaps Switzerland was the source of the latter-day Lemons.

(•♦•)

Rosebery Place was one of the two nicest streets in town. Tree-lined and backing onto a ravine, it was named for Archibald Primrose, the Fifth Earl of Rosebery, prime minister of the United Kingdom for a brief year or so in the late nineteenth century. His name lives on in many places around the world, like sylvan Rosebery Place.

Our house was the last of a short stretch of modest Edwardian houses – mostly two-storey foursquare redbrick buildings. Number 12 was only a storey-and-a-half tall, clad in wooden shingles painted French gray, with white trim and a red asphalt shingle roof. Some thought it was quite a bit older than the other houses on the street, and perhaps had been moved there in the early twentieth century and modified with its shingles and broad front porch. My high school history teacher Paul Baldwin has done research on the local architect John Findlay and credits the renovations to him, but the double front door and elaborate interior wooden mouldings were clues to its earlier age. During an aspirational phase in my misguided teens, I persuaded my parents that it needed white shutters, just like the fancier Colonial Revival house next door. In a recent visit I noticed that not only was the house still there but the shutters were also. I cringe now, knowing that they certainly do not belong.

Inside there was a long, narrow living room (originally two smaller rooms), then a dining room that opened to the "back room", which my parents added in the early 1960s when the family had expanded to six. Today it would be called a family room. The tiny kitchen had a small stove, scant counter space and no dishwasher. Upstairs were three bedrooms and one bathroom. Peter and I shared the front room and Paul and David the middle room, which is where, years later, Mom sat as I dressed her for Dad's funeral. At the back was my parents' bedroom, looking south over the backyard.

Our front porch was well used and provided a great relief during the humid days of summer in southwestern Ontario. Facing north, it was cool in the evening, with some privacy provided by the giant, deep green, heart-shaped leaves of Dutchman's pipe vines – *Aristolochia macrophylla* – that grew up the white-painted latticework.

Metcalfe was the other lovely street in St. Thomas. This was where my mother's older sister, my aunt Marion, and her husband, Don McDougall, lived, in a Gothic Revival house that dated from 1875. It had not one but three steeply pointed gables and elaborate fretwork verge boards. The

house sat across from the leafy Court House Square, and in the winter, when the trees were bare, it was visible across the Elgin Street ravine from our front porch. I often escaped the chaos of my home and the torment of my three brothers to spend time watching Uncle Don restore his house. Invariably, as I ventured to his basement woodworking shop, Aunt Marion would issue a stern warning to be careful.

The architectural legacy of these streets spoke of St. Thomas's prosperity in the late nineteenth and early twentieth centuries as a railway nexus. At one time, four main railroad lines passed through town, and many grand buildings related to the railway industry are the legacy of the town's advantageous location deep in southwestern Ontario and halfway between Buffalo and Detroit. The passenger station of the Canada Southern (later New York Central) Railway still stands as one of Canada's most prominent Italianate buildings, over 100 metres long.[3] The L&PS was the short rail

3 St. Thomas's railway history is shown in an excellent video "Railways of St. Thomas Elgin" produced by the Elgin Historical Society.

line that connected London with Port Stanley on Lake Erie, transporting goods and summer passengers to Port's beaches in its heyday.

My interest in architecture and history was sparked by my early exposure to these surroundings, and it was further encouraged by Uncle Don. Watching him as he stripped layers of faded cabbage-rose wallpaper from the hallway and restored the walnut detailing on the bannister of the serpentine staircase gave me respite from my life at home. Woodworking was his hobby, his own escape from his job as an account manager at Timken, one of the big employers in town, which made ball bearings for the automotive industry. Uncle Don also restored furniture and clocks and collected Ontario antiques and glassware, some of which I have inherited. As a child I often accompanied him and Aunt Marion as they scoured estate sales across Elgin County, while my brothers played football, volleyball, or basketball.

Uncle Don's brother, Clark McDougall, was an artist who worked alone in the basement of the house he shared with his mother on Inkerman Street. With acrylics, Clark created vibrant black-outlined canvases of rural Elgin County and street scenes of St. Thomas, Toronto and Buffalo. Many of them are in the collections of the National Gallery, Canada Council Art Bank, Art Gallery of Ontario, Vancouver Art Gallery and Museum London. After his death, the estate was handled by Mira Godard's gallery, one of Canada's leading dealers in modern art, who placed some of his best works with savvy private collectors, including Henry Luce, of LIFE magazine fame. Clark's remarkable work belied the cramped quarters of his "studio" next to the oil furnace, where I watched as he methodically worked on the canvasses.

Before I departed to spend a summer in Paris in 1975, Clark sent me a letter with coloured sketches of the types of details I should photograph for him in case he wanted to paint the streets of Paris. He had thousands of slides of fields, barns, old houses, brooks, trees and leaves in Elgin County, but he was keen to see close-ups of things like manhole covers, light poles and park benches in Paris. That letter now sits in the McIntosh Art Gallery at the University of Western Ontario in London, where his archives and many of his drawings and paintings are kept. The catalogue of an exhibit of his art is called *Fugitive Light: Clark McDougall's Destination Places*. I did

procure for him the requested slides while I was in Paris, but sadly none of them were ever realized in his paintings.

(•♦•)

All the Lemon boys went to Wellington Street School, which was just one block away from our home. We all were taught grade five social studies by Miss Purdy. Such was the history of my family in town that my father had also been taught grade five social studies by Miss Purdy, likely in the same classroom. She lived by herself in a room in a turreted redbrick Victorian house that overlooked the schoolyard.

Wellington was one of three similar redbrick Romanesque Revival public schools in St Thomas dating from 1898. The local architect Neil Darrach designed them all, as well as the high school – St. Thomas Collegiate Institute – the city hall and the Carnegie library, all completed at the peak of St. Thomas's expansion in the late nineteenth century spurred by the railroads. Wellington occupied a full city block and was three-storeys high on a raised stone base, with a slate-clad hipped roof. It was laid out in a pinwheel configuration, with four classrooms per floor and central crossing halls and stairs. The GIRLS entrance was on the east and the BOYS entrance was on the west. Each of the twelve rectangular classrooms had seven large sash windows and a freestanding blackboard which divided the cloakroom from the classroom.

On the south side, overlooking the schoolyard was the "chute", a double-helix slide shaped like a silo, windowless, clad in silver-painted metal panels. This was not original to the building, but it had been added sometime later to serve as a fire escape, and it served as an emergency exit from the second and third floors. In September, at the start of the school year, two students – one per upper floor – were granted the privilege of being the first to slip down the intertwining slides, sitting on a mat, to clean the accumulated dust. All of the remaining students then got to enjoy the thrill of this emergency drill. One fall, I got to be the first for the brief

ride. At first scary (it was pitch-black inside), the slide quickly became fun, and I had the satisfaction of kicking open the metal doors with a bang and then sliding out into the daylight.

My high school, Parkside Collegiate Institute, was not nearly as convenient to attend as public school had been. It meant trekking two kilometres south of town, quite a change from the easy one-block walk to Wellington Street School. There was a bridge to cross over the nearby ravine, then down along Wilson Avenue past the Armoury and Memorial Arena, over several sets of railway tracks, past Elmdale Cemetery and the St. Thomas Curling Club to finally reach Parkside. PCI was a sprawling, single-storey building with no architectural distinction whatsoever. But it was brand new, having been built just two years before I started grade nine, and spread out over a broad stretch of former farmland.

High school was a wretched time for me, and for that I lay part of the blame on the soulless character of the building. The sprawling single-storey building had only a few classrooms on the perimeter and those had just one window, positioned so that only the teacher could see outside. The building was the product of a time when school planners thought that views would be a distraction to students, and fresh air from open windows was considered old-fashioned. Nonetheless, the building was quite up to date, with a large auditorium, a theatre, band room, gymnasium, science classrooms, woodworking shops and auto repair shops, all spread out around the central atrium. This large space had a central fountain, sadly lacking a skylight, and was where everyone crossed paths during the school day. It was also where our prom was held.

At Parkside I was in the last of the grade ten Latin classes in Ontario, taught by Mr. Brown who had also taught my father Latin at St. Thomas Collegiate Institute decades earlier. I don't think Latin declension tests had changed very much over the intervening years. It did not take long for my classmates to notice that during our snap quizzes in class, Mr. Brown would read the questions in precisely the same order as he had taught them. If during the quiz he missed one word, we would quickly raise our hands and point out the omission.

While I did quite well scholastically, socially high school was five years of humiliation. Not at all athletic – aside from curling and a bit of volleyball – I was fearful of PE. As I was over six feet tall, it was assumed I would excel at basketball, which could not have been further from the truth. (I still have nightmares of the verbal torture Mr. Donahue inflicted on me.) I did enjoy being in the school band, even though I was assigned to play the tuba, which was chosen for me by Mr. Radlowski at the beginning of grade nine because I was the biggest kid in the class. After school, drama class and prom decorations were my extracurricular activities. My campaign for school council president failed, probably because of my last name. It was just too easy to tag my posters – featuring doctored Sunkist lemon ads – with "*DON'T* Vote for *A* Lemon".

Despite my social awkwardness at PCI, there were academic highlights, the best being an excellent teacher of grade ten history. Paul Baldwin was tall and lanky, looked studious with his dark-rimmed glasses, and was a gifted teacher. While some of my friends took copious notes of every word he said in class, often copying them out again at night, he urged us instead to jot down keywords. I suppose that was rather progressive of him. Most importantly, he had a special interest in local architectural history. As a bonus, he augmented the standard Canadian history curriculum by showing us slides of some of the oldest buildings in Elgin County that he had researched, some dating to the very early nineteenth century. I was fascinated.

When Parkside Collegiate Institute was assembling a team for the regional Reach for the Top TV quiz contest, I was chosen along with three others, and Mr. Baldwin was our coach.[4] During the taping of our match at the CFPL station in London, we were up against a school from the big city (there has always been a David and Goliath relationship between St. Thomas and nearby London). Our underdog team lost, but I did manage to beep and correctly answer most of our team's questions. I was particularly proud of knowing that Simon Fraser University was in Burnaby, not Vancouver, as the Central Collegiate kid had wrongly answered first. Perhaps that foreshadowed my interest in architecture, as I knew that SFU was designed by Arthur Erickson, one of Canada's premier architects.

Going to high school in southwestern Ontario meant going to the Stratford Shakespearean Festival every fall to see a production of the play we were studying that year in English class. Along with busloads of students from across the province, I saw *Hamlet, The Merchant of Venice*, the Scottish play, *King Lear* and *Othello*. Instead of writing an essay for an assignment in grade ten, I talked my teacher into letting me submit an almost-scale model of Tanya Moiseiwitsch's famous thrust stage at the Festival Theatre which I made of cardboard and balsa wood, and spray-painted with bronze automobile paint. It was done mostly from memory and a postcard view of the stage.

After the agony of finding a date for the prom the year I was in charge of the decorations – "Paris in the Spring" was the theme – I skipped my own prom in grade thirteen. I was more than ready to leave 12 Rosebery Place and go on to university.

I guess my interest in the old buildings of my upbringing had made me interested in architecture. And while I had only a vague idea of what was involved in studying architecture, and scant information about the profession from the guidance counsellor at Parkside, I sent out applications to the schools of architecture at the universities of Toronto, Waterloo and Carleton, with a very meagre portfolio. My father, the engineer, even cautioned that architecture would be very hard.

---

4 Paul Baldwin went on to be principal of East Elgin Secondary School, then mayor of Aylmer, Ontario. He retired to Ottawa where he continues to research the architectural legacy of St. Thomas.

In the fall of 1973 I headed east to the nation's capital to begin my studies at Carleton. It was at that time that I stopped being called Rob and became Robert.

Five decades later my brothers still call me Rob.

(•♦•)

During the six years I attended Carleton University, I returned home, usually by bus – a tedious twelve-hour journey – for holidays and two summers working in the office of a local architect. My brothers were all at university too – David at Guelph studying sciences, Paul at Wilfrid Laurier in the arts and Peter at Western studying photography. My parents remained a constant at 12 Rosebery Place, proud to have all four boys away at school and relieved that three of us graduated in the same year.

Age took its toll on my parents as they remained in the house they had lived in since just before I was born. Mom became frail and exhausted through the demanding years of looking after my father, who suffered first diabetes, then some heart problems, and finally the first signs of Alzheimer's disease. His huge frame shrank, and he moved from hospital to care home to another hospital in London. When he died in April 1997, I was in the air flying from Vancouver to see him; my brother Peter met me at the London airport with the news. When I dressed Mom for Dad's funeral, I realized how much she had worn away, having struggled to look after him all those years.

Mom carried on alone for five more years at 12 Rosebery Place, where she had lived almost her entire adult life. Suffering silently from a series of tiny strokes and heart problems, she refused home care of any kind and kept navigating the steps down to the dank basement to do her laundry. Just as she could always tell from the tone of my voice in our weekly phone conversations when something was bothering me, I could sense her being evasive when I asked if she were eating well.

She ended up in the local hospital, and when I visited her there, she would eat only if I fed her. From there she went to a nursing home where she lasted only two weeks, sharing a sterile room with someone she did not know, a sad diabetic woman with an amputated leg. Surely no one would choose to end their life in such circumstances.

(•♦•)

I think of Mom often. In September every year I make a version of her "chili sauce", a kind of sweet/savoury tomato relish that I am sure came from an early edition of *The Joy of Cooking*. It fills the house with the most wonderful smell – the cloves and allspice I think – and triggers a back-to-school sentiment that reminds me of St. Thomas. The year before Mom died, I called her to get the recipe. She recited it from memory, listing off seventeen tomatoes, peeled and chopped (she meant large ripe field tomatoes, but why seventeen, I have no idea), five green peppers, four sweet yellow peppers (she meant Hungarian peppers), four large onions – all chopped – simmered down to half, then brown sugar, vinegar, cloves and allspice. I have adjusted her recipe to add some hotter peppers, peppercorns and ginger, but I still label the jars "Norma's Chili Sauce". It is especially good with scrambled eggs, a grilled cheese sandwich, or macaroni and cheese, made with aged white Ontario cheddar, if I can find it. Just like she always used.

(•)

5TH

FIFTH YEAR PROJECT: "REANIMATION
IN THE CITY".

Three former school buildings in
the Dalhousie area of Ottawa are
regarded by students for potential reuse in other forms. Students aim to meet the needs of
this changing community with a
large ethnic group in the low in-
come sector.

New uses will hopefully bring
about a new vitality to the neigh-
borhood and thereby "reanimate"
the city.

After analysis of the three buildings, students select one site
and generate proposals for building and land.

Fifth year students may also
choose an independent study in
the Research and Development
field, under the tutelage of
Architectural professors.

Perspective rendering by Ira
Schachner, *below left*, of his
work on St. Jean Baptiste.

below right, introductory
drawing to project by Lesley
Till, showing map of Dalhousie
area and the three schools.

Top left, interior perspective
by Brad Abbott for his proposal
which includes housing and commercial.

Top right, Robert Lemon's proposal for a library.

Left photo of model by John Clark
for his Research and Development
proposal, an alternative design
of the Eaton's (College St.)
site.

Below drawing by Chris Posner of
one school, Our Lady Of Perpetual
Help, Eccles Street.

Below, a fifth year "crit" in
progress.

REANIMATION IN THE CITY

Dalhousie Ottawa

3 Schools

PENTRY LANE

THE INTERVIEW DID not go well. I had high hopes of attending the University of Toronto, where my father had studied engineering, despite having done very little research into the architecture program. So I really had no idea what should be included in a portfolio, how to prepare for an interview, or how to approach the application process.

On reflection, my portfolio was an embarrassment. It had a sketch or two of old houses and a few floor plans I had drawn on gridded paper of what I thought a perfect house should be. The symmetry, centre halls and formal rooms were no doubt based on the Andersons' Georgian Revival house at 24 Rosebery Place, my favourite house located just down the street from ours in St. Thomas.

It was the spring of 1973. My father was keen to drive me to Toronto and he waited in the car, parked somewhere along College Street, while I went inside for the interview. There were three parts to the interview, one each with a student rep, a professor and the head of the school. Things went off track when the hirsute student rep – with his fringed vest and strands of beads he looked like he could audition for a campus production of *Hair* – asked why I had chosen to wear a tie to the interview? It was a bow tie, at that. And why did my floor plans have "rooms?" Open, flowing spaces without labels and flexible design were obviously preferred at U of T. The rejection letter was soon to follow.

We drove the two hours back to St. Thomas in silence, as I could barely speak, I was so embarrassed by the ordeal. Not an auspicious beginning to my attempt to leave home to study architecture.

My experience at the University of Waterloo, while not as traumatic, also yielded a rejection letter. But it did come with a consolation prize – *carte blanche* acceptance to any program I should choose, other than architecture. Since I had never been to Ottawa and knew nothing about the Carleton University's program I had foolishly rejected their letter of acceptance which was based solely on my high school grades.

I resigned myself to accepting Waterloo's offer, and by August was registered for their BA program majoring in geography. I would be a high school teacher, I thought, just like Mr. Jenkins, one of several high school teachers I had had a crush on. (Ever since then, I have had a fondness for corduroy jackets and slim woollen ties.) I had already found an apartment to share with other students from St. Thomas who were also headed to Waterloo for the fall session.

Then in late August I got a letter from Carleton, offering me a place in their inaugural program of Industrial Design. I really had no idea what that might entail, but the four-year program – two in the architecture stream then two with engineers, under the direction of Dutch designer Wim Gilles – seemed like the next best thing to actual architecture. Uncle Don thought it was worth trying. As a result of this hasty decision, and without even seeing the campus, I headed to Ottawa by bus, a twelve-hour journey from London, through Toronto and Peterborough, to the nation's capital.

While it had not been my first choice of school, Carleton University it would be. Nor was 31 Pentry Lane the first place I lived in Ottawa. That would come in my last years there.

Too late to be assigned to a dormitory on campus, I found a rented room with Mrs. Rose in her tidy house up on Bronson Avenue. As architecture students spent long hours in the design studio, I reasoned that I would be mostly on campus and not in the tiny room anyway. Then, by late fall, a room had opened up at Glengarry House on the main Rideau Canal campus, and I moved in to share a room in a six-student suite in an airless high-rise without architectural merit of any kind.

My roommate was peculiar. He kept his dresser drawer fastidiously organized, with socks and underwear carefully positioned by each day of the week. Outside in the shared lounge the other four guys partied. I took solace and silence in my headphones with spin after spin of Pink Floyd and Elton John on the turntable to keep me company at night. I survived that year and returned to St. Thomas to work for the summer for the sole architect in town.

(•♦•)

That first year in studio at the School of Architecture was a revelation. The building itself had opened just a few years earlier and was radical in many ways that I did not appreciate at the time.

The first director of the school, Douglas Shadbolt, had commissioned Carmen Corneil to design a spare industrial building, rather like a warehouse or factory. In form, its four storeys stepped up and projected outwards to a flat roof, all supported by exposed concrete piers and deep concrete beams. Like many other buildings on campus, it had dark purple vitrified bricks but here they were large five-by-eight inch blocks laid in a distinctive bond pattern.[1] The windows were black painted steel.

Inside, there were exposed concrete block walls, concrete floors, black metal railings and brightly coloured mechanical pipes. It was intentionally left unfinished, in the words of the architect, to inspire creativity. The design preceded the high-tech inside-out Pompidou Centre in Paris by a decade. The building was organized around two interior streets, one at grade and the other at the fourth-floor studio level, with the Pit – a sunken

---

1 The architect's specifications call for "ironspot" blocks from Colonial Clay of New Brighton, Pennsylvania.

amphitheatre, two and a half storeys high – at the centre of the main floor. The Pit was the agora around which most activity in the building focussed. The director of the school could look out the interior windows of his office to see what was happening there. A sense of openness pervaded the place, and networks of stairs crisscrossed the interior, rather like an Escher drawing, which encouraged the interaction of students, professors and staff. I came to enjoy spending time in this concrete beehive of activity.

As a first order of business, our freshman class had to learn how to draft. Although I had seen my father's drafting board and drawing equipment in his land surveyor's office, with his pens, French curves and scales, I had never thought of learning how to draft from him. Perhaps I needed to leave home to discover the techniques of drafting on my own.

Professor Don Westwood was patient and precise in showing us how to set up our drafting boards with a T square, a triangle, a mechanical pencil (with interchangeable leads of different hardness), scales (imperial and metric), an eraser and erasing shield. A wide soft-bristle brush was handy for sweeping the erasures to the concrete floor.

Professor Westwood showed us how to prepare our drawing sheets to be of uniform size and orientation, always having north at the top and a graphic scale along the bottom. We learned how to draw lines of differing weights to distinguish elements that were more or less important. When asked how to depict a staircase in the plan and to show whether it was going down or up (some drawings are marked with "dn" and "up", which of course can be read as the same thing if the drawing is upside down), his reply was crystal clear. He explained that a floor plan is a horizontal section through the building, three feet off the floor, and you are looking at it from above. So it is logical that the short section of a staircase that the section cuts through would be heading down and the arrow and annotation stated accordingly. I have always remembered that, and while one could argue that you go up the staircase, you also go down. I often throw a little fit when I see staircases labelled otherwise.

Learning to letter neatly was also a skill we learned. The vertical strokes of each letter were drawn along the straight edge of a plastic triangle sitting along the T square, and the curved part, say the bulge of a D, or the three fins of an E, are drawn freehand, all while moving quickly from left to right. Decades later, I would make a half-hearted attempt to learn computer-aided drafting, but it was too late. I still do drawings the old-fashioned hand-drawn way and take delight in the craft and finesse of the finished product, with neatly crossed corners, line weight used judiciously and shading done with a soft pencil. Then the drawings are scanned and sent to Wayne Tam, my architectural drawing guru, for him to digitize.

(•◆•)

The friends I met on day one in the studio were to be important through my early years at Carleton. Lisa had a crush on me while Gerry, Chris, Jane and I worked together on group projects as Morley Morris Lemon and Neff, perhaps a better name for a law firm or a country rock band than student architects. For a journalism course we prepared a mockumentary, a multi-projector slide show exposé on the humble potato chip. Jane's father owned the Hostess potato chip factory in Galt, Ontario (now Cambridge). Our cohort travelled there to chronicle the operation and make a part real, part wry account of the complexity and origins of the potato chip. We laboured over the presentation in the school darkroom, creating absurd photomontages of great works of art – Botticelli's Venus stood nakedly on a shell-like ripple chip, and in creating Adam, God handed him a salt-and-vinegar chip. In retrospect, I would have relished showing Washington crossing the Delaware in search of a ketchup chip or having Magritte's green apple replaced with a sour cream-and-onion chip.

All the titles had to be individually printed or typed, then photographed on the copy stand with negative film to create white letters on a black background, some of the lettering hand coloured on the slides with felt pens. Four projectors with four carousels of slides – stacked two over two – were carefully focussed and sequenced to have images fade from one to another and be synced side by side. Today it would all be done by PowerPoint. "The History of the Potato Chip" got rave reviews when it was presented in the Pit for our journalism class.

After the first year of the Industrial Design program, I was certain that I wanted to pursue the main architecture stream, and so I was granted permission to make the switch to the five-year Bachelor of Architecture program. In the end I spread it over six years, with a gap year out to work and two study-abroad sojourns. The first study-abroad experience was spending a summer in Paris studying art and architectural history, as noted in "De la Porte de Vanves à la Maison Prouvé", the second involved a term at the Architectural Association in London, as recounted in "43 Arkwright Road NW3".

For the summer of my third year, I was lucky to be hired by Heritage Canada; there I worked for Martin Weaver, a distinguished conservationist who would become my mentor. Canada's umbrella heritage organization is now called the National Trust for Canada, but I prefer its original name. I was given the task of assembling and producing a series of technical dossiers on a wide range of heritage topics. These were double-pocketed folios that were filled with reprints of technical articles on wood conservation, paint, roofing, masonry, windows, recording of historic buildings and other topics. The reprints came from various agencies in Canada, the United States and the United Kingdom, some being reprints from *Old House Journal* or *APT Journal*. My job was to sort out the list of topics, order and assemble the reprints, and prepare bibliographies on each subject. I found it fascinating, especially as I had to read all the articles.

After that summer, Martin invited me to take a year off from Carleton to join him working at Restoration Services and then later on the Dealy Island Archaeological Project, as related in "Dealy Island".

At the end of my gap year, I returned for my fourth year at Carleton and settled into a townhouse on Pentry Lane in Ottawa South with a revolving cast of housemates. The practical but pedestrian design of the row of twenty-three three-storey houses stretched down to the Rideau River in a straight line; the location was a short walk from the Carleton campus. I had taken a sublet from an American professor who was on sabbatical and who bravely entrusted his home and extensive classical record collection to a group of university students. By the second year of this arrangement, our group had

settled into a collective comprised of all architecture students. I lucked out with the largest room across the top floor, facing west with a view of the river.

Our townhouse at 31 Pentry Lane came with most of the professor's furniture, including elegant Hepplewhite dining chairs (from Philadelphia, his hometown) and a thirty-foot-long deep red vinyl beanbag "snake", which served as the sofa in the living room. After a long day on campus, I would come home, put Elton John or Neil Young on the turntable, open a bottle of beer and slump onto the snake. The snake also proved quite popular for the occasional parties our household would host. One of them, around Halloween, was dubbed "Saturday Night Hay Fever"; it featured bales of hay, garish carved pumpkins and other kitsch. Disco was at its feverish height in the late 1970s, and that's what was spun on our turntable that night.

Somehow the term at the AA in London had ignited a spark of inspiration for my last year. Looking back at my projects in the fall of 1978, I can also see the influence that Robert Venturi had on me. His book *Complexity and Contradiction in Architecture* had been reprinted in 1977, and I devoured every page of my copy. Postmodernism was peaking at that time, and Venturi and his wife, Denise Scott Brown, were the starchitects of that movement. In Postmodernism I saw an alignment of viewing

history and applying it to modern design that suited my thinking about old buildings. I knew of the masters from my architectural history studies, but Venturi's take on Borromini, Soane and Lutyens showed that their work was still influential.

For example, I can now see that influence in my "Country House" project in the fall term. Having studied Venturi and Scott Brown's stylized take on a modern villa in their Brant House in Greenwich, Connecticut, I clearly used that as a reference for my Postmodern Ontario farmhouse. My model shows an assemblage of differently shaped rooms behind a bright redbrick façade. It's no secret that many Ontario Gothic houses out in the country have a formal front door that is never used, and often there were no steps ever installed; everyone used the more practical back door to the kitchen. So I had a ghost of a front door, and the real entrance to my design was through a broad, practical rear porch that served as the summer kitchen. There was a screened porch too, something remembered from Aunt Jean's cottage as noted in "Orchard Beach", and a feature I have since incorporated into a modern vacation house in the southern Gulf Islands of British Columbia.

By the spring term, the final studio assignment was to study the Dalhousie Ward in west Ottawa and imagine an architectural project there. I chose to repurpose a redundant early twentieth-century school to become a community library. Part of the project involved researching the historic typology of libraries, and I found similarities between such diverse land-marks as Paris's Bibliothèque St Geneviève, the Boston Public Library and the diminutive Carnegie library in St. Thomas, Ontario. All of the libraries had a large reading room on the upper floor, with broad windows high up to light the room and slender windows below, in between the stacks. I reinterpreted this big-over-small window pattern in designing new fenestration for the old school and signalling, if subtly, its change of use.

(•♦•)

Having weathered many scholastic years of enduring all-nighters immersed in the architectural studio, for my final year I vowed to head home at midnight. Very little was ever produced at three in the morning except piles of erasure dust from drawings done at the wrong scale. The studio was crowded and noisy with a blare of cassette players and transistor radios tuned to different stations. And the place was a mess, the floor piled with discarded paper, cardboard, food scraps, cigarette butts and the detritus of drawings. I ended up doing most of the work in my room at Pentry Lane and enjoyed the quiet and lack of distraction away from the studio.

So I was rather proud that my submission, completed during waking hours, got a glowing review during my final crit. The "crit" was the dreaded critical review of projects. Professors and students gathered around the work that was pinned up on the wall, and each of us had to explain what their project was all about. Usually the project would have been finished in the wee hours of the morning just before presentation. After a quick shower and lots of coffee, it was showtime. But I had finished on time and was quite composed and confident for the presentation.

All our projects had to be displayed on the walls of the upper street of the school. We had strict instructions to limit our panels – all uniformly sized – to twelve, plus a model. I chose to arrange eleven boards in a grid, leaving the bottom right spot for a model with the base the same size as a drawing. The model sat flush to the wall while I delivered my presentation during the crit. Then, at the end, with a flourish, I propped up the model on a wooden dowel so it could be viewed at eye level. The professor was impressed. It had taken me six years to learn that the skill of an architect is as much about how the idea is presented as the idea itself.

For that project, in addition to a Bachelor of Architecture degree, I was rewarded with not one but two prizes: first, the Ontario Lieutenant

Governor's medal for top standing in the class of architecture; and second, the Heritage Canada's Student Design Award, for which I was chosen as a co-winner for projects from schools of architecture across Canada. That award was a two-week trip through Britain studying Arts & Crafts architecture, which I undertook in the fall of 1980.

On convocation day, we hosted an after-party at 31 Pentry Lane. It happened that the son of Pierre Berton, a noted chronicler of Canadian history, was in my class, and he was dating the daughter of Maureen Forrester, Carleton's honorary degree recipient that year and one of the world's renowned mezzo-sopranos. So our modest student celebration, featuring strawberries dipped in sour cream and brown sugar, was graced by the presence of not one but two notable Canadians. It was quite a treat to see Pierre and Maureen gossiping in the kitchen or drinking beer from bottles as they sat on the crowded steps of 31 Pentry Lane.

Later in June my parents joined me at Queen's Park, Ontario's legislature in Toronto, the day I received my medal from Lieutenant Governor Pauline McGibbon. I think they were quite proud of my achievement.

During the summer of 1979 I worked on my résumé, intent on finding a job in Toronto, but to no avail. Then late in the summer I got word from John Davidson, the architect who had grown up in one of the nicer houses on Rosebery Place offering me a job at IBI Group in Vancouver. Supported by the Canadian government, I moved all my possessions (including the red vinyl snake I had purchased from the landlord at Pentry Lane) to the west coast. I would spend the next four decades there in my career as an architect.

(•)

DE LA PORTE DE VANVES À LA MAISON PROUVÉ

MEREDITH SAID THERE would never be a gap in the flow of traffic. She was right. A steady stream of Peugeots, Renaults and Citroens as well as BMWs, Mercedes and the odd Volvo was weaving in and out along the vast stretch of pavement, all at breathtaking speed. There were taxis, scooters, motorcycles, vans, trucks, tour buses and an occasional ambulance or *voiture de police* with sirens blaring.

"Take a deep breath, thrust out your left arm, stare down the first car that comes your way and step off the curb", she said. Like ducklings we followed in line behind her. The cars did indeed slow down. We carried on bravely, crossing the twelve lanes of ferocious traffic to reach the obelisk in the centre of Place de la Concorde. Then we repeated the sequence with right arms out as we carried on across the remaining twelve lanes of traffic to land at the Champs Elysées, where we rewarded ourselves with giant *coupes St. James* smothered in *chantilly* at Le Drugstore.

This and other adventures occurred during my first trip to Paris in the summer of 1975 studying art and architectural history under the guidance of Meredith Sykes.

Learning how to cross the road was not one of the things I had expected to learn that summer. But that and other adventures stick in my mind more than the specific art treasures in the museums and galleries we toured. I wasn't so much interested in the history of the Winged Victory of Samothrace (Greek, second century BC) as I was impressed by its dramatic placement on a pedestal at the top of a flight of stairs in Le Louvre. And while I did pen a paper that summer comparing Manet and Monet, my indifference to the topic was sadly evident. It was rubbish.

Studying architecture at Carleton gave me the bonus of taking courses in other disciplines on campus, and I always looked forward to the days when I would head to the Arts Tower for the slide lectures that Meredith Sykes gave on the history of Western art and architecture. So in my second year, when she announced a summer school credit course in Paris, I gave notice for a hiatus from my summer job at Bruce Martin Architects in St. Thomas and departed for six weeks in Paris.

Right away we had to learn how to navigate the Metro system as our digs, a spartan hostel at Centre Didot in the unfashionable fourteenth *arrondissement* of southwest Paris, was at the end of the "Invalides–Porte de Vanves" subway line. The area near the station displayed very little in the way of Parisian charm, but its mix of immigrants supported a vibrant street market and plenty of cheap meal-ticket cafés made it liveable.

It did not take long to figure out the vast and efficient Metro. Some stations still had their elaborate Art Nouveau cast iron entryways that dated to the opening of the system in 1900. While many cities grew and expanded in the twentieth century, the population of central Paris remained the same, even dipping slightly from the 2.2 million people who lived there when the Metro opened. Still, it is a testament to the foresight of the system's designers that stations were located within a five-hundred-metre walk of anywhere. Today, the idea of a walkable city seems new, but in Paris it dates back a century and a quarter.

And walk we did. We trooped endlessly along the grand boulevards, the back streets and the network of glazed *passages* that thread through the city. We learned all about Haussmann and the rebuilding (razing actually) of Paris in the late nineteenth century, and the reason behind *les Grands Boulevards*. Meredith showed us the views of the city from the rooftop of La Samaritaine department store (now a posh hotel), from the Basilica atop Montmartre, and from a great distance at the newly built La Défense.

Our group spent every weekday with Professor Sykes, visiting art museums one day and taking long walking tours to explore the architecture of different *arrondissements* the next. We toured galleries large and small. I loved the Rodin Museum and its gardens, and the Musée de Cluny with its catacombs. We saw *cloisonné* enamels, and the Jeu de Paume and Monet's water lilies at the Orangerie.

We visited Le Louvre several times and once had a special tour of the conservation labs in the attic suite of rooms that overlook the Seine. There we learned how paintings were cleaned with painstaking patience using Q-tips, and how *lacunae* (small losses in original paint areas) were filled in with tiny parallel brushstrokes so as to keep the new work distinct, at close range, from the original. That concept applies to architectural conservation too, where new work is to be distinguishable from, but compatible with, the original. And all of it reversible, so that it could be removed without damaging the original material.

I had the letter, illustrated with little coloured sketches, that Clark McDougall had written to me showing the things he was curious about – drain covers, benches, advertisements and leaf patterns of trees. His insight sparked my curiosity about street details. I was fascinated by the dark square cobblestones laid in a diagonal pattern to give better stability for wheeled traffic, and the graceful rows of linden trees overhanging the Seine, sheltering the bookstalls. Looking back at my slides of that trip, I found many images with details of such things, and I was grateful for the focus his suggestions had given me. Clark never did paint Parisian street scenes, but I think he would have been fascinated by the colours and textures of the city, much as he had been drawn to the bright lights of downtown Buffalo or Toronto, especially reflected on rainy pavement.

(•♦•)

Food figures prominently in my life. Memories of meals and markets form a thread through many chapters of my memoir, but my expectations ran particularly high for my first trip to Paris – platters of oysters, *coq au vin* served in copper coquettes, *tarte tatin*, runny cheeses and good wine. But as students, we learned to survive on budget meals and developed a fondness for the baguettes lashed with *moutarde* (free) that were provided when I ordered a small salad or an omelette for a meal. Often we dined at the hostel with indoor picnics of baguettes, cheeses, *pâté* and bottles of cheap wine from the local shops at Porte de Vanves. We never had *macarons* at Ladurée, but we did line up for *crème glacée* at Berthillon on Île Saint-Louis. There was an automat-cum-cafeteria on Boulevard Saint-Germain, where I tasted *tripes* for the first and last time.

Nor did I dine at La Tour d'Argent or any place with a Michelin star, but I do remember, not Proust's *madeleines,* but eating at Chartier in Montmartre. Meredith took us there as much for the splendid, if faded, Art Nouveau room as for the simple and cheap food. The tables were packed tightly together, covered with paper, and the floor was crunchy with baguette crumbs. Brusque, portly waiters with stained white aprons served the simple bistro fare with *vin ordinaire* sloshed in sturdy tumblers from litre carafes. I believe Chartier is rather more refined these days, but it is still one of the oldest and most beautiful restaurants in Paris.

We took a trip to Versailles, where it rained the whole day and we could only visit the gardens, as the palace was undergoing restoration. In fact, I have been to Versailles several times but for various reasons I have never set foot inside the palace. We went to Chartres, saw the palace in Fontainebleau and other châteaux in Île-de-France, including Vaux le Vicomte, Chantilly and Malmaison along with their splendid gardens. There were weekend excursions to Giverny and the beaches of Normandy, where Meredith deftly showed us how to change into a bathing suit on the beach while wrapped in a large towel. I never thought that such a skill would be a valuable memory of studying architectural history. We visited St. Malo, Mont St. Michel, and I ate

moules frites for the first time. For a souvenir I bought a navy and white striped woollen *Mariniere* with buttons on the shoulder.

It is the little things that make the greatest impression, and I am thankful to Meredith Sykes for encouraging my keen interest in travel, cities, art and architecture. And also for teaching me how to cross twelve lanes of traffic and to disrobe in public.

I thank her for another bit of sage travel advice. She told us that whenever we become weary of walking the streets of a city, we should find the nicest hotel in town, walk into the lobby with a confidant "I belong here" air, plunk down on a plush sofa or gilded fauteuil, rest our feet and people-watch. If anyone asks what we're doing there, she advised us to say, with a bit of hauteur, that we are waiting for Mr. Hyde-Smythe or Madame Chareau (or any other pretentious-sounding name). She guaranteed that we would be left in peace. A decent shopping bag, from say Au Printemps or Galeries Lafayette, helps as a prop. Just leave the backpack at the hostel.

(•♦•)

This trip was only the beginning of my experiences in Paris and France. There was another short visit to Paris as part of a Eurail backpacking tour of Europe in 1977 when I saw the newly opened Centre Pompidou. I was in Paris again for a stopover before the term at the Architectural Association in London that is related in "43 Arkwright Road NW3". Our class of fourth-year Carleton architecture students spent New Year's Eve of 1978 in the City of Lights. Our cheap charter package from Ottawa had us posted in a dreary hotel near Gare du Nord, but we brought in the New Year with a splendid dinner at Le Procopé in Saint-Germain, beginning with oysters and ending with baked Alaska. At midnight we started a drunken traipse along the Seine and on to the Champs Elysées – kissing a handsome gendarme along the way – before collapsing in our hotel. The next day we took the train to Calais for a stomach-wrenching ferry ride to Folkestone and then on to London.

(•♦•)

The best visits to France would happen later, in the company of Agnès Cailliau. She is an architect I met when we studied architectural conservation in Rome, and our shared interest in the architecture of Carlo Scarpa had blossomed into a great friendship. In the course of her career as a restoration architect, Agnès lived in Paris, Compiègne and Nancy. She also taught at the architecture school in Rouen.

Paris was not the only part of France that I saw through Agnès's eyes. After our studies in Rome in 1984, I was invited to join her family at their summer home at Le Cap Bénat. The low-slung modern bungalow was set amongst the pine trees of a rocky promontory, just south of Bormes-les-Mimosas. I saw the French Riviera in a rustic and natural light without the flashy trappings of the rest of the Côte d'Azur. Mornings were spent swimming in the sea, then an alfresco lunch with her large family – often a simple roast and a tomato salad with torn basil leaves, washed down with jugs of local rosé – followed by an afternoon nap during the heat of the day.

In the late afternoon, Agnès, her partner, Paul, and their infant son, Côme, and I would head out for an excursion to visit historic monasteries in the south of France.

A year later my partner Bob Ledingham and I were invited to a Sunday lunch at her parents' home in Fontainebleau. They lived in a sprawling historic farmhouse, probably dating from the eighteenth century, that had been beautifully restored as a family home. The stone wall of the former barn was tight to the road and we entered through a wooden gate into a gravel courtyard, flanked by the long range of the stone house. The house's *enfilade* of rooms opened to a broad lawn that reached down to the river Loing, where we strolled after lunch.

Agnès comes from a family of some distinction. Her father, Pierre Cailliau, was a presence. Tall, elegant, with striking square glasses and perfectly bilingual, he headed INSEAD, an international business school in Fontainebleau in the 1970s, and was a nephew of Charles de Gaulle. Her aunt had a sprawling flat overlooking Piazza Navona, where Agnès lived while in Rome. Yet she had no pretentions as a result of her upbringing. She was tall, willowy, with cropped graying hair, and dressed simply but stylishly. Slim jeans and a loose top would be paired with a bright scarf and always very good shoes.[1]

(⋄◆⋄)

On visits to France in later years, Bob Ledingham and I would be treated to several special tours of historic sites that Agnès had arranged through her work as a restoration architect for des Bâtiments de France. We were privileged to take a hard-hat tour on the scaffolding of the limestone restoration of la Cour Carrée du Louvre while it was officially closed. Then we toured an entire street of modernist houses named for Robert Mallet-Stevens, the architect who designed them, whose work in the late 1920s and early 1930s was no doubt the inspiration for the Barber House, our own Art Moderne house in Vancouver.

---

1 Bob and I took her shopping on rue du Cherche-Midi for apple-green Robert Clergerie boots as a thank-you gift for her hospitality.

But it was her entrée to five very special houses of the early twentieth century that was the most fascinating and influential for me. Agnès opened the doors for private tours of houses designed by Le Corbusier, Edwin Lutyens, Alvar Aalto, Pierre Chareau and Jean Prouvé.

The first special tour happened the year after my studies in Rome. Bob and I met Agnès and Bente Lange, another ICCROM colleague, in Paris. We planned to head out to Poissy to see if we could visit the Villa Savoye, perhaps the best-known work of the Swiss architect Charles-Édouard Jeanneret, better known as Le Corbusier or simply Corbu. His Villa Savoye is one of the most famous buildings in the world, remarkable for its modernity and inventiveness when it was completed in 1931. It is so iconic it was modelled for a LEGO set. I was given one for a gift, and its instruction book runs to eighty-six illustrated pages. Raised above the ground on stilts – *pilotis* was what Corbu called them – the ascent to the main floor is accomplished by long ramps, brightened by light filtering down from an upper terrace.

With great optimism, we set out to have a look at the place. Although it was officially closed for restoration, somehow Agnès, with young Côme in tow, managed to charm the caretaker into letting us look inside. What a treat to see the original mosaic tiles being restored, historic plaster wall colours reinstated and the steel windows being repaired.

On another trip, and knowing of my interest in English Arts & Crafts architecture, Agnès had arranged for a visit to le Bois des Moutiers, Sir Edwin Lutyens' only work in France. Our private tour was given by the owner, Madame Mallet who insisted on first showing us the splendid view of the English Channel from her bedroom. The house, tall and square and quite plainly clad in roughcast stucco with a red tile roof, sits high above the coast with a steep lawn in a clearing between dense deciduous woods, descending to the water. The large, but by no means grand, house was finely crafted in 1898 and reflected Lutyens' growing reputation as the master architect of the English country house. Le Bois des Moutiers would have been right at home in Surrey, but instead was situated on the coast of Normandy, near Varengeville, hardly a location where one would expect to find a fine Arts & Crafts country house and garden.

A splendid double-height music room with tall mullioned windows would later inspire my design of a house for a client in Vancouver. The walled garden, again with handsome rough stucco walls and fine brick fillet detailing, designed by Gertrude Jekyll, was a hortensia-lovers delight. Vast plantings of rhododendrons and azaleas thrive there.

Just as le Bois des Moutiers was Lutyens' only building in France, Maison Louis Carré is the famed Finnish architect Alvar Aalto's only building on French soil. This late 1950s house sits on a large property near Bazoches-sur-Guyonne, about forty minutes west of Paris. Carré owned a notable gallery of modern art in Paris, so having a modern house in the country – as much a gallery as a residence – designed by the famous Finnish architect must have been quite remarkable for the Parisian art set.

Hardly French in any way, it has all the hallmarks of Aalto's buildings in Finland: white painted brickwork, copper detailing and wooden framed windows outside, and terra cotta floor tiles, leather detailing, wood panelling, cobalt blue wall tiles and custom light fixtures and furnishings within. Now a museum, the house retains Madame Carré's possessions just as they were in 1996 when she died, including her Chanel suits and bespoke luggage with decals from her world travels with her husband. There was a bottle of vintage 1959 Riesling on the kitchen counter, the date of the house's completion.

On another occasion in Paris, Agnès arranged a private tour of La Maison de Verre, completed in 1932 by the designer Pierre Chareau as the home, studio and office of a gynaecologist, and often cited as one of the most complete and remarkable interiors ever created. Aptly, the facades of La Maison de Verre are made almost entirely of glass blocks. It is surprising to encounter the house in a modest courtyard in Paris's seventh *arrondissement,* not as a stand-alone building but actually the rebuilding of the lower three floors of a rather ordinary apartment building. The glass blocks cleverly light the interior while concealing the distractions of the unremarkable views outside.

The house was still privately owned and occasionally lived in by the doctor son of the gynaecologist who had commissioned the house. The interior is a wonder of exposed steel beams, custom metalwork, glass and custom furnishings. There are tapestries and screens by Jean Lurcat, articulating cabinetry, even plumbing fixtures that swivel. Rubber floor tiles, custom-made for the house, are hardly what one would expect a bourgeois Parisian household to have had at that time.

But the best was saved for last. At the end of my summer in York in 1998 (as recounted in the chapter "Castle Howard's End"), Agnès invited me to stay with her in Nancy, that elegant city in eastern France, where she was living in Jean Prouvé's own house in the hills above the city. Jean Prouvé was a *constructeur* – part engineer, part self-taught architect, industrial and furniture designer – in Nancy, once the capital of the Duchy of Lorraine, and an important centre of Art Nouveau design. Emille Gallé is a native son. Prouvé's base in Nancy became a place of experimentation in construction and modern design. As part of her job with les bâtiments historique de la France, Agnès had the opportunity to live in Prouvé's own house, now owned by the city of Nancy, with the obligation of over-seeing its conservation.

My journey to Nancy started very early in the morning at York Station, where I caught the express train to London Kings Cross, followed by several Tube rides to Waterloo Station for the Eurostar to Paris Gare du Nord. There was just time for a *croque-monsieur* and a Kronenbourg at a sidewalk café before walking to Gare de l'Est for a fast train to Metz, where Agnès had arranged to meet me. On the last leg of the trip, I changed into proper clothes in the train's WC for an evening reception she had invited me to. Then it was a short drive to Nancy, before I collapsed into bed at midnight. Swathed in vintage shell-pink monogrammed linen sheets that had belonged to Agnès's mother, I had the most profound and restful sleep that I can ever recall.

When Agnès went to work the next day, I had the house to myself. Maison Prouvé represented the experiments of its celebrated designer. Prouvé's ideas – ship-like bulkhead doors, heated concrete floors, aluminum panelled exterior cladding, exposed steel framing with articulated trusses, enormous pivoting metal-framed glazing – were explored in his design for the house that he built in 1954. The house also boasted many pieces of original Prouvé-designed furnishings, now much coveted and copied.

(•♦•)

The six-decade period between 1898 and 1959 produced a remarkable collection of private homes in France representing the work of five great designers, not one of which could be considered typically French. But they all show the commitment of their owners to design and experimentation that is a legacy of the relationship of both owner and designer. I am indebted to Agnès Cailliau for opening the doors of those houses to me, and for those lovely sleeps in her mother's linen sheets at Maison Prouvé. Later in my architectural practice, which included many custom residential commissions, I repeatedly tapped into my mental library of images of the works of Aalto, Chareau, Lutyens, and Prouvé for design inspiration.

There is one other memory of visits with Agnès that stand out: the lesson of navigating a proper French cheese course.

(•♦•)

There are very strict rules about cheese, at least as I learned them from Agnès. Eating Sunday lunch at her Paris flat meant visiting a *fromagerie* that morning and watching as she negotiated with the proprietor over the selection. There would be seven cheeses for the four of us. Agnès was asked if the *Camembert* was for lunch that day, supper that night, or for the next day? There would be one ripe for each occasion. There were butters to choose from, scooped from crockery urns, two from Normandie and two from Bretagne, each a slightly different shade of creamy pale yellow.

After a simple lunch of *rosbif* and *salade,* and with decent wine still left in our tumblers, the cheese was presented on a plain board. We could choose as much as we liked of any or all on offer. There was always a bit of butter on the baguette before the cheese. But Agnès's strict rules meant only choosing once (no double dipping) and never taking the nose. The nose, or tip of the wedge of runny cheeses, is the prized part that no one ever takes. The nose is left for the table. I took the nose once and learned from Agnès's slight gasp and brief look of disappointment that I had committed a serious *faux pas*. I have never done that since.

(♦)

43 ARKWRIGHT ROAD NW3

"GARDEN FLAT IN HAMPSTEAD" read the ad in the January 1978 *Time Out* magazine.

That flat was to be my address as part of a group of twenty Carleton students who spent a term abroad at London's Architectural Association. The AA is a famously radical school, housed in a series of handsome Georgian townhouses at 32 Bedford Square. After a flight to Paris (the cheapest way across the Atlantic), where we brought in the New Year, and a turbulent ferry trip to Folkestone, we were left to our own devices for our first assignment in London: find a place to live. I had no idea what attending the AA or living in London would entail.

My sharp-eyed classmate Richard Lindseth had found a flat in north London, a short walk from the Hampstead Heath underground stop. He rounded up four of us to share cold-water digs occupying the ground floor of a redbrick Victorian terrace house at 34 Arkwright Road. We had two rooms to ourselves: a lounge with twin sofa beds for the girls, opening to the rose garden; and the front room for the boys, facing the road. We shared a frigid bathroom and kitchen with others in the building – there was frost on the inside of the windows each morning. The only heat for the shivering months of January, February and March was the gas fire in the lounge, which was fed by ten-pence coins, and there was no hot water for bathing other than a coin-fed water heater. We worked out a plan whereby we could afford bathing every other evening, the girls sharing the bath water in sequence on one day, then the boys on the other day. The nearby Tottenham Court Road YMCA provided a place for hot showers and exercise. And we frequented the bar at the AA as a place to have a pint and a sausage roll, and to chat with other students.

Once we were settled, we took the Northern Line from Hampstead to the Tottenham Court Road station then walked the short distance to the AA on Bedford Square every day for school, where we attended lectures and workshops that expanded our exposure to architectural thought and theory. We learned first-hand about Pop, Brutalism, Archigram, the Smithsons, James Stirling and Denys Lasdun, and we read the works of Kenneth Frampton and

Charles Jencks. Some of the buildings I had already seen in the slide library at Carleton, where I had had a part-time gig sorting and filing the collection. But it was all rather bewilderingly futuristic to me. I signed up for the Friday curriculum of historic preservation, where I learned about medieval timber framing, and at the Building Centre gallery next door I explored a seminal exhibit on "The English House" which would plant the seed for my later studies. I could not help but notice the similarity between Lutyens' house, called The Salutation, and the Andersons' house at 24 Rosebery Place.

As poor students, we had scant opportunity to take advantage of all the arts and culture that London had to offer. I discovered the cabinet of curiosities that was Sir John Soane's house museum in Lincoln's Inn Field, and we did manage to take in some theatre, films, concerts. I admired the brutalist beauty of Lasdun's National Theatre, then just two years old, and went there as much for the building as the drama. We made excursions to Hampton Court, Windsor and Bath.

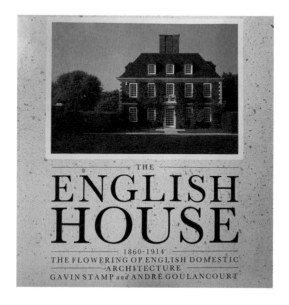

(◆)

Once the term was over in late March, I spent two weeks hitchhiking across Ireland with my friend Earle Briggs. We endured frigid nights in hostels and survived on the kindness of the locals and a diet of tinned sardines and crackers. The occasional B+B afforded a chance for a warm bed, a bath and a decent breakfast. But it was memorable nonetheless to see Baltimore, stay on the island of Sherkin, tour the Ring of Kerry and visit Clifton. We celebrated St. Patrick's Day in Dublin. I think the tally for the cost of the trip was something like sixty-five Irish pounds. Total. I kept one of those Irish pounds as a souvenir, the design was so beautiful.

(•◆•)

That study term was not my first visit to London, nor the last, but it was when I spent the longest time there (and had a mailing address). The first visit had been with my grade twelve high school English class during spring break in 1972. We had a ten-day agenda of theatre performances and tours of literary historic sites. In researching this memoir, I found a yellow plastic box of faded Kodachrome slides that had not been opened in the intervening forty-nine years to revive my recollections of the trip. Especially exciting was the flight on a chartered BOAC 747 jumbo jet from Toronto's Malton (now Pearson) Airport. The jumbo had first flown commercially the year before, so it was still quite a big deal, especially for my father, the air force navigator, who drove me to the airport. The seats in all classes of service were occupied by students from all over Ontario, and as luck would have it, I got to sit up front in First Class. I got first-class service too (I think there was a trolley with carved roast beef), and for a long time I kept as a souvenir the BOAC champagne glass and linen napkin that just happened to slip into my carry-on bag.

We made the rounds of must-see sites like the Tower of London and its jewels, ate at Ye Olde Cheshire Cheese, saw the homes of Thomas Carlyle and Charles Dickens and visited Madame Tussaud's. We sat through the tedium of *The Mouse Trap* (by then already tired in its twentieth year) and saw Alec Guinness in *Voyage Round My Father* at the Haymarket Theatre. Just before nodding off during that performance, I recall hearing the sage

advice to always sleep on your right side so as not to put pressure on the heart on the left side. I do not remember much else.

(◆◆◆)

Having won the Heritage Canada prize for my Carleton final year studio project, I was the recipient of not just a medal but also a two-week trip to Britain, which I took in 1980. The British Council planned an itinerary to tour the Arts & Crafts architecture of Edwin Lutyens, C.F.A. Voysey and Charles Rennie Mackintosh.

I have had a keen interest in Lutyens, particularly since I encountered his mannerist Arts & Crafts architecture in Robert Venturi's *Complexity and Contradiction in Architecture*. His Deanery Garden was the subject of an essay and a series of drawings for a class assignment I completed at Carleton. While on that trip in 1980, I saw many of Lutyens' buildings, including Munstead Wood, the home he designed for the famed gardener Gertrude Jekyll in Godalming, Surrey. Munstead Wood stands as the epitome of the Arts & Crafts country house and garden. My volume of *Houses and Gardens by E.L. Lutyens* features photos of it on the dust jacket. When I showed up unannounced on the doorstep, Lady Clark was gracious enough to invite me in. It was a privilege to walk through that house, with its complex arrangement of spaces and carefully detailed nooks and fine craftsmanship. Looking out through mullioned casement windows to see first-hand Jekyll's splendid garden – so influential in later garden theory – was an additional treat. I added my name to the guest register a page or two after the signatures of Philip Johnson and Vincent Scully.

Voysey's work was of interest to me too, as there is a direct connection between his office and that of an architectural firm in Vancouver. The paper I wrote as a summary of the trip noted the link between Voysey and Cecil Croker Fox, who left Voysey's office to come to British Columbia when he

went to work in the office of Samuel Maclure.[1] I visited Voysey's own house, The Orchard at Chorley Wood (1900), which was the clear inspiration for the almost identical Huntting House in Vancouver's Shaughnessy neighbourhood that was designed by Maclure and Fox (1912).

For the last stop on that trip, I took the train to Glasgow to see the work of Charles Rennie Mackintosh. Coincidentally, there was a festival of his work that very weekend. I was entertained by experts, including the director of the School of Art, who gave me a bolt of the fabric Mackintosh (or perhaps his wife, Mary Macdonald) had designed for the curtains in his office. I toured most of Mackintosh's buildings in and around Glasgow, including the Willow Tea Rooms, Scotland Street School and his townhouse, which had been relocated to the Huntarian Museum. The Hill House in Helensburgh was a special treat, with its chalky white *harling* stucco exterior and splendid pale, almost iridescent, interiors. Every surface, stick of furniture or light fixture had been designed by Mackintosh or his wife Mary.

Years later I had the delight of staying at Hill House, in the upper floor suite of rooms that had once been the nursery, when it was available for holiday rental through the Landmark Trust.[2] My interest in establishing a similar trust of historic houses in Canada for holiday rentals was sparked by that stay at Hill House. One day my place in Stratford seven&nine may be part of such a Trust.

(• ◆ •)

Later, Bob Ledingham and I had regular summer visits to London for interior design shows or antiquing, or as a stopover before performances at Glyndebourne. Bob's design trips meant exploring shops and studios in Chelsea, Kings Road and Pimlico, and needless to say, our accommodations on those trips were much more comfortable than my cold-water flat in Hampstead. We stayed with friends in their flat in Bayswater and later at a townhouse in Notting Hill. We also booked suites at posh hotels in

---

1 Maclure was a prolific architect in British Columbia in the early twentieth century, with offices in Vancouver and Victoria.

2 The Hill House is owned by the National Trust for Scotland and the nursery suite is no longer part of the Landmark Trust's inventory.

Mayfair and Knightsbridge. For a few years The Dorchester was our favourite, until they replaced the ecru linen sheets (with red piping) with cotton, the gilding in the lobby became blinding and we learned that the owner, the Sultan of Brunei, had started chopping off the hands of homosexuals in his kingdom. The Berkeley was more quietly elegant and had the bonus of a rooftop pool. The tiny, exquisite Blue Bar, with its walls of *craquelure* lacquer in Sir Edwin Lutyens' signature shade of gray-blue, was the perfect meeting place for a martini with London friends.

We spent evenings at the Royal Opera House, Covent Garden, English National Opera, and Sadler's Wells. My friend Earle Briggs' career focussed on theatre design, and his connections opened the door to a backstage tour of the Savoy Theatre in all its aluminum-leaf Art Deco splendour. (The powder room at the Barber House is clad in aluminum leaf as a nod to the Savoy). Our friend Jean Hodgins arranged tickets to an intimate chamber music recital in Christopher Wren's Royal Hospital Chelsea.

We never tired of visiting Sir John Soane's Museum and often took friends there to show them the room with the hinged panels that display a set of Hogarth's *A Rake's Progress* paintings. We brushed up on British history at the National Portrait Gallery, followed by lunch at Portrait overlooking Trafalgar Square. Bob's bespoke John Lobb oxfords, which I still have, meant fittings at the shop in St. James's Street over three visits to London.

We almost always booked a table for lunch at The River Café, notwithstanding the sticker shock of the bill for the wood-fired Dover sole. But meeting the owners Rose Gray and Ruth Rogers, and having their signed cookbooks, brings back memories of those Italian meals in the modern dining room overlooking the Thames, next to the offices of Ruth's architect husband Richard Rogers. We also enjoyed memorable dinners at St. John (pigs' tails and teal), Lindsay House (roasted veal sweetbreads), Scott's (fish pie), Bluebird (steak tartare with a raw egg yolk, shortly after mad cow disease was over), Bistrot Bruno (prosciutto-wrapped cod with lentils) and Zafferano's (chilli crab linguine). Some of these dishes I have attempted to replicate at home over the years, although never the pigs' tails.

After Bob died, I inquired of Lobb's about having his wooden lasts returned as a keepsake. In proper British form, they replied they would be happy to part with them for a substantial fee. I was perplexed at what value bespoke shoe moulds could possibly have to anyone else and presume they are sitting on a shelf in the back of the workshop gathering dust. Or perhaps they have been repurposed as the lasts for some other gentleman's custom shoes.

(• ♦ •)

In the past decade, now travelling alone, I saw a chance to see different sides of London. For one trip, instead of booking a hotel, I looked to Airbnb for digs for a four-day stay enroute to Rome, where I planned to celebrate my sixtieth birthday. I scrolled past dozens of similar, anonymous-looking flats until one entry caught my attention: a "narrow-boat long barge" rental in Bethnal Green. I would have the entire boat to myself, moored on the Regent's Canal in northeast London, under the bridge bordering Hackney. Decades ago, including my time at the AA, I would not have ventured to

E2, but now it is alive with galleries, good restaurants and hip coffee shops while still retaining much of its gritty patina.

The Regent's Canal snakes its way across the top of London, with several operating locks that provide a navigable route for watercraft through a fascinating swath of the metropolis. The footpath that lined the northern edge of the canal near my barge was packed with commuting and recreational cyclists, walkers and runners. The sounds of bike bells and ducks splashing on the canal were the most noise I heard on the barge during my stay, notwithstanding the traffic on the Mare Street Bridge with its bus traffic literally overhead. With Victoria Park just a five-minute walk from my watery digs, and London Fields and the London Lido – with an outdoor fifty-metre pool open year-round – I had plenty of options for exercise.

Getting on and off the barge was a tricky dance of balance and resolve, requiring that I navigate a wooden ladder and gangplank which was anchored precariously to the edge of the canal, then hopping over the neighbouring barge to the deck of mine. But once I was on board, the domicile was stylish and very comfortable with all the *mod cons*: a tiny shipshape kitchen, proper head (bathroom) and cozy bedroom. There were lots of books and even a little wood stove to take off the dampness.

I ordered my morning coffee at the uber-hip Hackney Bureau just across the bridge – so hip, in fact, there wasn't even a sign. Nor was there a sign for Bistrotheque, a smart restaurant upstairs in a cavernous warehouse space just a block from my barge. Broadway Market was a short walk away, with its bustling high street of shops, where I had several *macchiati* at Climpson & Sons. The Bethnal Green tube stop, on the very convenient Central Line, was quite close by. A longer walk took me to Columbia Road for a dinner of steak tartare one night at the bar of Brawn. Spitalfields spiffed-up market and namesake church, plus a St. John outpost for nose-to-tail eating, were not far away. This part of London is worth visiting again. But one caveat: staying there comes with the caution that getting to and from Heathrow by cab is a convoluted and expensive drive through vast parts of the metropolis. When CrossRail is finished, it should be more accessible.

Not two months later that fall, I was back in London before a visit with my friends the Hodginses in Dorset. This time I booked a stay at Durrants, a small historic hotel in Marylebone. Until then I had not thought much about the area and was pleasantly surprised by how hip, yet charming, it had become. On past trips, the area had been *terra incognita*, just north of Oxford Street and below Regent's Park, with Baker Street and Portman Square being the only reference points for me. But in between is a very lovely area with townhouses, noted medical facilities in Harley Street and a vibrant high street.

I was as intrigued by the history of Durrants as I was by the location. A privately owned hotel fashioned from four handsome Georgian townhouses on George Street, it is both stylish and well worn. The ancient wooden staircase in the lobby creaks with comforting satisfaction at every footstep. Rare these days is a hotel that has real keys, and at Durrants the keys are substantial. Their thick brass handles and broad rubber protector ring are designed to be practical when the key is dropped in the wooden box at the porter's counter on departing for the day. The porters are prompt in proffering it back upon one's return.

Durrants is across the street from the Wallace Collection, which was conveniently open the morning I arrived with time to kill waiting for my room to be ready. In the hotel is a tiny wood-panelled bar with a roaring fireplace, the perfect cozy spot for a martini. And once, just once, I had breakfast in the stylish Grill Room, where the table was laid with a crisp

linen cloth and polished silver, the setting for absolutely the most memorable plate of soft scrambled eggs piled on layers of Scottish smoked salmon.

Happily, there was a decent Italian bakery café around the corner on Marylebone High Street, where on most mornings I would have a *macchiato* and a decent, if simpler, version of scrambled eggs with smoked salmon. Marylebone is the home base for the Monocle publishing empire.[3] The small but stylish Monocle shop was just down George Street; that is where I picked up a clever map of Marylebone. I was soon heading to Chiltern Street to shop and to see the Chiltern Firehouse hotel, a splendid repurposing of a late Victorian firehouse. It seemed like one needed to be called David – Cameron or Beckham – to get past the doorman. They did let me in to have

3 Monocle is the publishing empire that started with *wallpaper** magazine.

tea one rainy afternoon. And I was allowed drinks at the posh bar on another visit, but there was never a table available for dinner.

Close by was Wigmore Hall, which is remarkable for its fine acoustics and noted musical programming. The Daunt Bookstore, specializing in travel literature, was just up the street. I went for morning runs in Regent's Park or Hyde Park, which are both almost equidistant from Durrants, and there was a convenient swimming pool at a gym on Baker Street, just two blocks way.

That visit was in November 2014, when the impressive display of 888,246 blood red ceramic poppies which filled the dry moat of the Tower of London to commemorate lives lost in World War I was worth jostling with the crowds to see. I was fortunate to obtain a last-minute ticket to a performance at the National Theatre. The National is always worth a visit, as much for its brutalist architecture, now seeing a revival in interest and its concrete restoration, as for the playbill.

Then after some early Christmas shopping, lunch at Ottolenghi's NOPI and purchasing some sliced-to-order smoked Scottish salmon at Selfridge's Food Hall (better than Harrod's or Fortnum & Mason in my opinion), I was on the train to stay with the Hodginses in Dorset, one of many visits to the county, as I recall in "Wessex".

(• ♦ •)

There is something about London that I think makes it the most interesting city in the world. In the arrivals hall at Heathrow, I can feel that I am in a global city, as Hugh Grant said in his voiceover in the opening credits of *Love Actually*. London has the Heathrow Express, the Underground, the best cabs anywhere, lovely parks and squares, and rows and rows of handsome terrace houses. There is a vibrant cultural life, with perhaps the best music and theatre in the world, modern design and revered history, and very good food if you know where to look.

Whether it is in Hampstead, Bedford Square, Bethnal Green, Bayswater, Notting Hill, Mayfair or Marylebone, I have seen how liveable London's terrace houses are. Rows of identical buildings are distinguished by customized front-door colours, all with rear gardens and many with mew houses behind along the rear lanes. That form of housing should be the future for cities like Vancouver that are searching for more density, not just in condo towers but in a civilized, neighbourly way.

Should an opportunity arise to take a sabbatical anywhere, I would choose London as base and Marylebone as the neighbourhood. For now, Durrants is my first choice of digs in London. No one makes a more luscious mound of soft scrambled eggs with smoked Scottish salmon. The quietly elegant walnut-panelled Grill Room, with its austere painting of a greyhound looking down on the room, is the best place to start the day before exploring some of what London has to offer.

(♦)

DEALY ISLAND

I T WAS MESMERIZING to watch the tundra that stretched below us on the flight from Yellowknife to Resolute Bay. The shimmering lakes and streams looked like quicksilver that had been dripped over the land, and the lack of trees made the shiny water stand out even more in the bright sun and flat terrain. This was my first taste of the vastness of Canada above the Arctic Circle, the second part of a journey that began in Ottawa and ended on tiny Dealy Island, way up north at latitude 74.9N.

My summer job in 1978 was to be the photographer for the Dealy Island Archaeological Project, living in a tent on that desolate island overlooking Viscount Melville Sound.

The final leg of our journey was in a de Havilland Twin Otter airplane. Landing was a white knuckle affair, as the stony beach had quite a rake to it and hardly seemed to be the length of a proper runway. But the Otter is nimble and sturdy, a remarkable achievement in aeronautical design. Equipped with

either pontoons or fat tires, it can take off and land just about anywhere. It is the one-ton truck of northern aviation, and proudly Canadian.

Captain Henry Kellett's journey to Dealy Island with his British naval party on HMS *Resolute* – which set out in 1853 in search of the Franklin Expedition – was no doubt much more arduous than our trip 125 years later. His legacy was Kellett's Storehouse, a stone cache of goods and supplies intended to keep the Franklin crew alive, should they find it. It is now an historic site and has suffered badly from vandalism, freeze-thaw decay, polar bear pilferage and souvenir hunters.

(• ♦ •)

I was heading north because of Martin Weaver. Martin was my mentor and an architectural conservator, and he invited me to join him and a team of archaeologists and conservators for four weeks of research, recording and conservation of the stone storehouse, midden and artefacts that Captain Kellett and his crew had left behind.

I first worked for Martin Weaver as a summer student at Heritage Canada in Ottawa. When he left to work for Restoration Services (then a division of the Department of Indian and Northern Affairs and now Parks Canada) to write the first of a series of books on Canadian architectural conservation, he asked me to join him to help with the book. I took a deep breath and decided to take a gap year from Carleton to work for the federal government, the first of my experiences working for government bureaucracies during my career.

Bureaucracies are legendary for working at a glacial pace and being filled with "lifers". But Restoration Services was different, staffed with a very talented and experienced group of professionals including architects, engineers and conservators. All conducted research, wrote scholarly articles for technical journals and passed along their knowledge by teaching.

Martin was very highly regarded in the field of conservation, not just in Canada and his native England but internationally. Like me he had studied at the AA in London. He taught at Columbia University, and later split his time between Ottawa and New York when he was not working on projects just about anywhere in the world. For my architectural practice in Vancouver, I invited him to consult on the conservation of a stone and terra cotta building that I was overseeing.

At the offices of Restoration Services, Martin was sequestered in a boardroom on *charette*,[1] hammering out page after page of material related to the history and conservation of wood in Canada while I was beavering away on the bibliography. Word processing was in its infancy in 1977, and all the entries in the bibliography had to be coded on punch cards by keywords, meaning that I had to read all the books and journal articles and decide on the keywords. I learned a lot about marine borers, wood rot, dendrochronology and historic timber framing that year. The bibliography extended to seventy or so pages and was arranged alphabetically by author and by keywords.

That work term led to Martin's inviting me to join him on the Dealy Island Archaeological Project. I doubt I would have had the opportunity to experience Canada's High Arctic if I had been accepted at the schools of architecture in Toronto or Waterloo.

(•♦•)

---

1 *Charette* is a term used for an intense period of design or planning activity focussed on a single topic without outside interruption.

On Dealy Island, my role was to record, in photos and drawings, the progress of the archaeological dig at Kellett's Storehouse. The structure had been built of stone, wood and canvas in 1853 by the crew of a British Royal Navy expedition. Kellett's was one of twenty-four such parties that set out in search of the lost expedition of Sir John Franklin, which had disappeared in 1847 while searching for a Northwest Passage. In 2014 and 2016, Franklin's sunken ships, the *Erebus* and the *Terror*, were found, 160-odd years later, not far from Dealy Island.

The archaeological project was sponsored by the Prince of Wales Northern Heritage Centre in Yellowknife. Preparations had begun in the summer of 1977, when Martin's scouting trip determined that Kellett's Storehouse needed an archaeological and conservation team to record and protect the vulnerable remnants. A detailed plan was made by Brian Yorga, Charles Hett and Martin Weaver. The archaeologists would recover samples of historic artefacts to be conserved on site before being transferred to Yellowknife for further research and conservation. Repairs would be made to the cache's stone walls, a seasonal stream would be diverted and all the work would be photographed in stages. Finally, an insulated wooden floor would be constructed to protect the remains in situ until a full archaeological dig could be undertaken.

All people and supplies had to fit in the de Havilland Twin Otter. The workhorse plane ultimately made three trips to deliver everything to the tiny island. This meant procuring the supplies necessary to retrieve, record, conserve and protect the relics. For our four-week stay, we needed gear to set up three separate camps, one each for sleeping, working and eating, separated by a great distance due to the threat of polar bears. There were piles of tents, cots, sleeping bags, stoves and kitchen kit, food rations, conservation materials, coolers, dry ice, cameras with two kinds of film, a bipod, a tripod, masonry tools and all the material to make a temporary insulated floor out of timber and plywood, pre-cut in Yellowknife to fit into the Otter.

We also brought a dog to alert us to the presence of polar bears, and rifles to protect us from them. Before leaving for Dealy we all took rifle lessons. I had never fired a gun before and thankfully did not need to do so in the Arctic, nor have I used one since, but it was reassuring to know that I could, should the need arise. The kit also involved the right clothing, including a bright orange anorak which I wore every day and have only recently retired, and, of course, stout boots. In preparing this story, I dug deep into a cache of old slides that had been stored for almost five decades in the cardboard box that originally contained my Greb Kodiak insulated

work boots, size twelve. I wore them every day on Dealy Island, and for many years later they were my dedicated gardening boots at Estergreen.

We had to learn to live together, sleeping in one tent with no privacy whatsoever, and adjusting to the complexities of working in a harsh climate. Ablutions were of necessity rudimentary. There was fresh water in a tiny lake above the shore cliff, which we used for drinking, cooking, weekly sponge baths and cold-water shaving. For bodily functions we waded into the frigid waters of the strait and relied on the prevailing tides to flush things away.

In July the sun never sets at that latitude, so our internal clocks had to be reset. We relied on an alarm clock to get up in the "morning". Breakfast involved coffee and freshly made bannock, a kind of biscuit bread made by Charles Hett in a cast iron frying pan, and usually smeared with peanut butter. Though other details of the meals have escaped my memory, I do recall a special treat of fresh steaks that were airdropped by the crew of a flight heading north to a gas field up on Ellesmere Island.

Although it may have been austere, the forlorn landscape of Dealy Island, just south of Melville Island and overlooking the steely blue waters of Viscount Melville Sound, was breathtaking. In this formidable place, for the very brief six weeks of "summer", a remarkable range of wildflowers bloomed – there were tiny versions of purple orchids, arctic poppies and cotton grass.

Such was the historic interest in Dealy Island that a stone cairn at the top point of the island, 180 feet above sea level, contained notes from past visitors, including one from then prime minister Pierre Elliott Trudeau, who had stopped on the island as part of his tour of the High Arctic in 1975.

(•♦•)

Our plan for the month was first to divert a stream that was eroding the walls of the cache and then to reset the fallen stones back into the wall. Then the artefacts were removed from the uppermost, semi-thawed pile inside the stone walls of the cache. The archaeologists would record the location of each object relative to a string grid set up over the site. The objects, including bits of blue serge uniforms, rifles, leather boots, cast iron stoves, bags of coal and some of the thousands of cans of food, would be handed to the two conservators to record, treat and pack in their working tent for later transport back to Yellowknife.

As the photographer for the project, I was taught scaled-rectified photography by Robin Letellier at Restoration Services. The stone walls of the building were recorded using a Super Cambo 4X5 camera with a 135mm lens. The camera was tilted to the slope of the wall and had a special grid

on the lens that enabled the photos to be scaled. The archaeologists' work of removing layers of artefacts within the walls had to be recorded from above. This was well before the age of drones, so there was a complicated arrangement to erect a Whittlesey Foundation bipod to hoist a camera thirty feet above the site. Both large-format film and Polaroids were used. I had to store the films inside my anorak so my body heat would keep them warm. The daily temperature was usually 6 to 8 degrees Celsius, with a very high relative humidity of 70 to 80 percent.

Vandalism at the Kellett's Storehouse site had escalated with the increase in oil and gas exploration in the Arctic in the previous decades. Before that, most visitors were polar bears rummaging for food amongst the ancient tins that had been left there by Captain Kellett. I found the cans fascinating, with labels still legible a century and a quarter later. One read "tripe and onions". The cans were sealed with lead, and it is thought that many of the British naval explorers died of lead poisoning from the cans.

My log of photographs and a set of record drawings were finished later that summer when I was back in Ottawa. They contributed to a scholarly paper that we presented at an archaeological conference the following spring, which was my first chance to travel to my future home in Vancouver.

(• ♦ •)

On a recent trip to Ottawa, I was allowed to see some of the artefacts that were removed from Dealy Island in 1978. They have had quite a journey, having been taken first to Yellowknife for conservation and storage. In 1999 the new territory of Nunavut was created, which included Dealy Island. The artefacts then became the property of the Government of Nunavut's Department of Culture and Heritage. In 2016, 941 of the artefacts collected during that summer were shipped to a conservation facility in Gatineau, Quebec, near Ottawa. The items include a coal-burning cast iron stove, whole barrels, half a barrel top inscribed "cocoa", a pair of woollen mittens, long underwear, socks, leather boots, wool uniform fragments, numerous barrel staves, empty food cans, strapping, cordage, buttons, canvas and wool fragments, animal bones, bottle glass and wood from crates and nails.

Before my visit to Ottawa, I had sent the Nunavut conservator the photo of our team on Dealy Island taken on July 23, 1978, the 125th anniversary of the completion of Kellett's Storehouse, and asked her if some of the items depicted in the photo could be opened up for me to see. Joanne McInnis was kind enough to retrieve and show me some of those items that had not been seen in forty-three years – even by her. She opened up crates containing a wooden barrel marked "potatoes" and the cast iron stove seen in the photo. Smaller items had been carefully and individually packaged in foam cradles lined with acid-free cotton and tied with cotton ribbons; it was quite an unveiling. I was especially thrilled to see, in a box marked "978.36 Dealy Island", a rusted but unopened can with an intact paper label that read "Tripe and Onions preserved by Jackson Hogarth & Co. Aberdeen".

It is staggering to think that one can, filled with just enough food for one meal for two hungry seamen, was once part of a shipment of thousands of tins that were sent from Britain almost 170 years ago to feed men lost in the Arctic. As I viewed these objects again, I thought of the determination of the nineteenth-century explorers to endure the extremes of the Arctic when they were so inadequately equipped.

(• ◆ •)

Martin also introduced me to APT, the international Association for Preservation Technology that he had helped found and for which he served as president for several years. In 1979 I was invited to attend their conference in Denver as the technical assistant, where I was in charge of the slide carousels for all the presentations. My experience organizing the slide library at Carleton came in handy when I had to figure out how to load a Kodak carousel in order to avoid upside-down or backward images. Later, in the late 1990s, I would establish a B.C. chapter of APT, which promoted conservation on Canada's west coast through lectures and tours.

I looked up tributes to Martin Weaver after he died in 2004. His obituary in the *New York Times* barely touches on the extent of his achievements in the field of conservation worldwide. I remember him as a gifted and animated man, eager to tackle any conservation challenge, be it fixing crumbling stone walls in the Arctic, writing a book about wood borers or advising on the very strange use of brittle terra cotta in an historic structure in Vancouver. I am grateful for the time I spent working under his supervision and for all I learned from him.

(•)

ESTERGREEN

J UST A MONTH after I met him, Bob Ledingham and I drove across the border from Vancouver to rural Whatcom County in Washington to a property he had recently purchased. I was a bit wary of this excursion, so early in our relationship. The border guards asked, "Where are you going and why?" And also, pointedly, "How do you know each other?" Our weasel answer was that we "worked together". Years later that would be true, but in the spring of 1981 we had yet to work together. I was pretty certain his intentions were above board, as I had already met his mother, but one does hear about people crossing the border and never being seen again.

Of course it all turned out fine. We toured the grounds of the five-acre plot that was set far off the road, up on a little hill, surrounded by rows of raspberry canes and next to a small lake that edged up into Canada. The mountains of B.C.'s Coast Range were located to the north, and majestic Mt. Baker peeked above the foothills to the east. The property had a large

plain gray stucco garage, two dilapidated wooden sheds that had once housed livestock, and a small house, more like a cottage, that was rather rundown. There were many towering cedar trees, old lilacs, a lopsided tree that had been grafted for two kinds of apples, and a wisteria vine that had smothered a wooden trellis. The place had seen better days.

At first Bob called it The Farm, but more often it was known as Mole Hill after the burrowing rodents that ruined the lawns. Finally, when we discovered the history of Andy Estergreen, the Swedish homesteader who settled there in 1882 and built a cedar plank cabin in 1887, we called it Estergreen. It became our weekend retreat from the city and the one constant home Bob and I owned over our almost thirty-two years together.

(•♦•)

Friends often ask how I met Robert Ledingham. He was a prominent interior designer, and I was an Architect-in-Training.[1] I had moved to Vancouver from Ottawa in the fall of 1979 to work for IBI Group Architects at their offices in a converted warehouse building in historic Yaletown.

---

1 AIT is the term given by the Architectural Institute of BC to young architects charting a course for registration in the profession.

My apartment was in the West End at The Americana, the flat furnished sparsely with items purchased at Karelia in Gastown to complement the red vinyl snake I had brought from Pentry Lane. By then I had finally figured out that I was gay.

No, Bob and I did not meet at some gallery opening, post-opera soirée or fancy dinner party. Our circles of friends overlapped a bit, and I had heard of him. We finally met on a Saturday night on the eve of Mother's Day in 1981 when I dropped by the Shaggy Horse for a beer.

The Shaggy Horse was a staple of the gay bar scene in Vancouver in the early 1980s, more pub-friendly than disco-like. I had been out for the evening with my friend Bill Reed, a noted landscape architect and the gay ex-husband of my best friend Val, who worked with me at IBI Group. Val sat right in front of me in the office and was the nexus of my new circle of friends. Once she realized that I was not boyfriend material, she introduced me to Bill, thinking we might click. We were not a romantic match but became great friends.

The "Shaggy," or the Chenille Camel as it was dubbed, had walls covered in shag carpet that reeked of cigarette smoke. It was arranged on two levels, with a sunken main floor and an upper balcony. Down the street in Yaletown was the fancier Gandydancer, more in tune with the peak of disco, which was the place I usually frequented.

Guys would enter the Shaggy, scan the room and either go down to the main bar or up to the balcony to survey the crowd from above. That night, Bill's back was to the door and he did not see the tall, handsome man with a full beard, wearing a plaid shirt, whom I noticed. That man went up to the gallery just after I first saw him. With a bottle of Old Style in my hand, I told Bill that I was going upstairs to see if he were still there. He was. Our eyes met, and I walked back down to tell Bill. Not long afterward, I told him that the handsome man was approaching us. Bill turned around and shrieked, "Oh, that's just Bob Ledingham"; of course Bob was his friend, an interior designer with whom he often worked.

A few weeks after we met, Bob invited me to his mother's apartment for Sunday supper. Eleanor had been widowed for decades when she moved to Vancouver from Saskatoon. The meal was pure prairie simplicity – baked ham, scalloped potatoes, curried peaches and ambrosia salad. That first night she offered me a drink before dinner, and I foolishly requested Campari, which of course she did not have. A glass of Dubonnet would be just fine, thank you very much. At the next Sunday dinner, I was surprised and touched that she had acquired a bottle of Campari just for me. I must have made a good impression on her.

Not long after, Bob and I went for that drive across the border to see Estergreen.

(•◆•)

Bob's last words before I left for Istanbul were "Don't buy a carpet". Then, on the penultimate day of a week at a heritage conference, having until that moment resisted the rug temptation, a charming salesman lured me into a shop to have some apple tea. I called Bob that night to tell him about the lovely ten-by-thirteen foot Turcoman Kandilli I had seen, and he said, "Don't buy the carpet". The next day I returned to the shop to say "no sale", but ended up coming home with the carpet neatly folded in my baggage. Eventually the rug graced the floor of the living room at Estergreen.

Such was the dynamic of two designers coexisting for more than three decades. I was the architect with an interest in historic preservation, and Bob was the interior designer with a discerning modernist eye. Imagine

Edwin Lutyens living with Florence Knoll. Our divergent design paths did cross on occasion, and we collaborated on several houses including the Barber House. But we relaxed both our design differences and our souls at our rural retreat.

Estergreen is so close to the Canadian border that cell phones think they are in Abbotsford, British Columbia. Andy Estergreen's old dairy farm had dwindled to just a five-acre patch, part garden and part pasture, with the original house and some outbuildings by the time Bob bought it.

After three renovations in as many decades, Estergreen's cottage charm had evolved to reflect our interests in Asia, Scandinavia and Canadiana.

For the final renovation in 2005, Bob and I expanded the kitchen, added a covered porch – perfect for morning coffee – and bay windows in the living and dining rooms. To replace the old ladder staircase to the upper floor, I had a local cabinetmaker build a Japanese-style *kaidan-dansu* step cabinet to store firewood and our collection of vases in its stacked chests. Rustic larch flooring was laid in most rooms, with travertine added to the hall and bathrooms. Finally warming to that Turkish carpet, Bob worked his magic on a colour scheme based on its rust and indigo tones – cream linen chenille on the sofa, indigo hemp denim slipcovers for the lounge chairs, ginger-coloured walls and walnut-toned linen drapery. A bit of Scandinavia was found in the Hans Wegner chairs that tied in with the vintage Royal Copenhagen dishes – cobalt and white – that were reserved for our best guests. My Ontario heritage showed in some Clark McDougall paintings and a Victorian gothic mantle clock my uncle Don had restored.

In the kitchen, an antique Japanese *mizuya* cabinet anchored one wall, and a sixteen-foot-long stainless steel counter, salvaged from a renovation for one of Bob's clients, spanned the southern wall, with a row of windows allowing views over the raspberry canes. Doors opened to the porch and sundeck. More doors connected the octagonal dining room, lined with flaxen-coloured linen drapes, to the decks.

The main bedroom was the opposite of Bob's modern aesthetic, but ironically reflected his Saskatchewan roots. During the first renovation, cedar planks and beams were discovered in what was the original Estergreen cabin. These were left exposed, and they became the backstop to an antique prairie bedstead, cleverly widened to queen size, that dominated the room. A prized Duncan Grant nude – a bit of Bloomsbury in the bedroom – seemed right at home.

The garden had its first iteration through the hard work of Bob's ex, Daryl McConnell, who shared Estergreen with us in the early years. Our friend Bill Reed devised a grand landscape plan, much of which was later realized. We had inherited more than the cabin from the old Estergreen farm: ancient apple, plum and pear trees; a gnarled wisteria and old lilacs; and towering conifers. Over time, Daryl and his weekend guests toiled to add peonies, lilies, masses of irises and a burgeoning vegetable garden.

Then the garden changed again, in response to my architectural eye. The lawns were levelled and edged with low concrete retaining walls, defined by hedges of box, ilex and Russian laurel and a handsome row of Katsura trees. The old wisteria was propped up by a pergola made of hemlock columns I had designed for the Canadian Craft Museum decades earlier, on a terrace of "carib brown" brick pavers (Bill Reed's favourite), edged with salvaged terra cotta blocks from Vancouver's Art Deco Georgia

Medical-Dental Building. Nearby, a large bronze basin, a souvenir of a trip to Jaipur, sat on the stump of an old mountain ash. That massive tree's fate was a topic of discord in our household. I loved the dappled shade, but Bob hated the mess of leaves and berries it dropped on the deck. He won, and the tree came down.

I laid out lengths of high fencing and an arbour especially for rambling heritage roses we purchased from Free Spirit Nursery in Langley. Tulips were Bob's favourite flower, but we never did much to plant them, instead favouring masses of daffodils that multiplied and spread in a woodland garden and flowered around his birthday in early March. Later, Daphne Frost helped with her keen eye for plants and colour, grouping and editing with great skill. She brought order to the peony border, adding a bed of *persicaria* and shapely cloud-pruned box hedging surrounding the cream-glazed pot in the front yard.

Our weekends at Estergreen usually began with guests arriving late Saturday afternoon in time for cocktails and a walk in the garden. Afterwards, everyone would gather in the kitchen around the central worktable, made for us from salvaged teak and fir beams, while dinner preparations progressed. Our entertaining routine had Bob tending bar and the Weber kettle grill while I manned the gas range. Music was provided by old vinyl, and we would listen to *Songs of the Auvergne* or Strauss's *Four Last Songs*, over and over and over.

Then there would be lazy Sunday mornings. Yet not so lazy as to miss a bracing run on the country roads or a bike ride, sometimes a long ride in the lower reaches of Mt. Baker (even up to the top one time, a 160-kilometre round trip), with stops for coffee at the many espresso huts peppered throughout Whatcom County. Then lunch, often an alfresco meal under the pergola, that could last all afternoon.

(•♦•)

After Bob's death in 2013, I continued to make regular weekend visits to Estergreen. The beauty of the garden and its rural surroundings had always been a great pleasure. I enjoyed more long bike rides on the rural roads, along with trips to Bellingham and excursions along Chuckanut Drive to purchase mussels and great bread in Edison. While I do not have a green thumb, I enjoyed working on the garden design and seeing the place change over the seasons. I watched the bed of daffodils I had planted for Bob spread and bloom.

One spring I spent a weekend alone at Estergreen. While harvesting early asparagus and rhubarb from the vegetable garden, I noticed the oddest thing under an old maple tree: a random cluster of seven tall, near-black tulips. I do not recall planting them. I brought the blooms home to Vancouver, and in a plain crystal vase they stayed, ramrod straight, in silent beauty until they finally faded, two years to the day after Bob died.

Yet the upkeep of a five-acre property is considerable, especially from a distance. Even with a weekly lawn-mowing service, a series of local gardeners, and Brandon, the builder who did repairs and kept an eye on the place, it was clear that maintaining this as a solo retreat was not tenable long-term. After 9/11, the border-crossing process had become increasingly complicated and unpredictable, and the uncertainty often deterred friends from Vancouver from coming for short weekend visits.

Eventually I decided I had to sell the farm.

It started with great promise, as my Seattle-based real estate agent thought the secluded location, rural setting, design pedigree and proximity to both Mt. Baker and Puget Sound would appeal to urbanites escaping Seattle, San Francisco or Dallas. She promoted the place internationally, and in early September, within one day of the listing going live, there was an attractive full-price offer from a couple in Bellingham, just forty minutes away.

It was too good to be true. They said they wanted everything included in the deal – almost all the furnishings and art – and would not bother with an inspection as they wanted a closing within weeks. But there were some strings that became hurdles (if I can mix a metaphor here) and other stipulations beyond my control.

They did not like to look at my neighbour's burn pile or the rusting carcass of an old Thunderbird that had been dumped in the back field years ago. Within days I had the car removed and approached the neighbours about their burn pile. The demands kept escalating as I dealt with a land title issue. The survey showed that some of the neighbour's raspberry canes extended onto the Estergreen lot, and I scrambled to get a written agreement to document that. Then there was the escrow process. Unlike in Canada, U.S. properties go through a protracted escrow review, where all the details of previous owners and sales have to be rectified. As the deed for Estergreen went back over a century, there were some errors to be corrected.

In order to comply with the short closing date, I had arranged for the removal of the few furnishings and the art the purchasers did not want to keep, and had them stored in the neighbour's barn across the road. All was ready in time for the couple's final walk-through with my agent the night before the closing. I left a bottle of Veuve Clicquot on the kitchen island as a welcome gift.

Later that night I got a distressing message from my agent. The couple had indeed done an inspection and finally disclosed that they had done an evaluation of the property and its contents. They decided to rescind their previous full-price offer and instead offer one-fourth of the value. They had also taken the bottle of Veuve Clicquot. My agent was distraught about the deal collapsing literally at the eleventh hour.

So was I. She retrieved the champagne

It took another year and two more offers before the property finally sold. The challenge of cleaning out three decades of accumulated stuff from the house, garage and outbuildings was a formidable task. For years the farm was the last resting place for old dishes, unwanted furniture and junk from our house in Vancouver or from well-meaning friends. In the era of CDs, we seemed to have amassed all our friends' old LPs. Much was donated to Habitat for Humanity, whose volunteers spent two days with several large trucks hauling away old furniture, dozens of canning jars, old building materials, rolls of roofing, wire fencing, garden tools and machinery. There was a chest freezer, still filled with frozen raspberries, plums and currants from harvests years ago, and two old refrigerators with more stuff.

My car was loaded with the last of the personal items from the house when I made my final trip back across the border, late on a Friday night. Rather than being whisked through with a carload of household effects ("chattels" is the term), I was interrogated by the border agent about the ownership of the goods. He wanted to see receipts for items decades old, including the Turkish carpet, and proof that I had inherited the farm. After an hour in the waiting room at the Aldergrove border station, and just about in tears, I was finally allowed through at midnight.

(◆)

I do wonder what happened to Estergreen after it was sold. My neighbour with the hazelnut orchard across the lake phoned me a year later to ask about the new owners, as he had not seen any signs of life on the property. I did not know, as I have not been back across that border since then. A recent Google Maps search shows there are still buildings there, in more or less the locations I remember them. So perhaps the legacy of Andy Estergreen remains, 134 years later.

Bob's obituary was featured in the national edition of the *Globe and Mail,* with a picture of him lying on a bench on the deck at Estergreen with our Scottish terrier Ginger perched on his chest. He seems content and at peace, and I like to remember him – and Estergreen – that way.

(•)

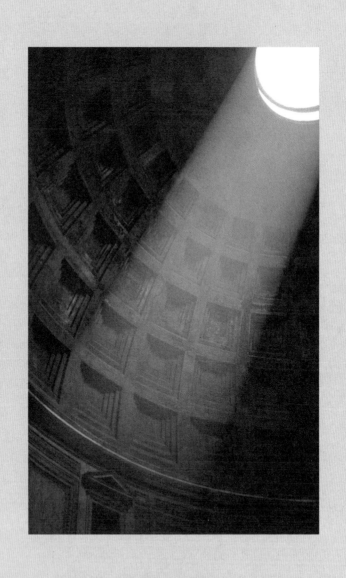

LARGO DELLA FONTANELLA DI BORGHESE

W ITH HER CROPPED red hair, freckles and ruddy complexion, and dressed practically in a linen shirt and chinos, Bente's Nordic appearance belied her knowledge of Rome's historic buildings. She had us looking up at the pale beige façade of the Palazzo Pamphili as she described how its colour had been restored to its original hue. We were in the Piazza Navona, on a walking tour with colleagues returning to Rome for a ten-year reunion of our conservation studies at ICCROM that had begun in January 1984.

My friend, the Danish architect Bente Lange, had found, in her decade of research into the historic colours of Rome, that the deep orange and ochre tones found throughout the *centro storico* were not original. They were the result of the gradual repainting of polluted and darkened stucco over time, and were also likely a political statement from the Fascist era of the twentieth century – Mussolini preferred the dark colours, as they reminded him of his rural village.

Bente's book *The Colours of Rome*[1] was the result of her studies of what Baroque Rome looked like. In it she wrote, "In contrast to the sky-coloured buildings of the Baroque, which seemed transparent, airy, light, floating, diffuse, soluble and intangible, the earthen colours made buildings appear robust, massive, strong, tangible and permanent". She researched *vedute*[2] of Rome in museums ranging from the Galleria Nazionale d'Arte Antica, Palazzo Braschi in the Eternal City to Copenhagen's National Gallery, the Boston Museum of Fine Arts and the Metropolitan Museum of Art in New York to study contemporary depictions of the city.

Those paintings indeed showed pale-coloured facades, the "colours of air". She then compared that evidence with paint samplings on the facades, scraping down layers of paint and lime wash in a technique known as a paint ladder, to show the earlier colours hidden underneath. In her book she offers a vivid example, using her own watercolour drawings, of how the twin buildings that flank the Spanish Steps, one now orange and the other pink, are a departure from the original vision of pale blue and beige. She has consulted on the restoration of many other buildings in Rome to get the true historic colours. The transformations have been stunning.

(•◆•)

It's odd that it took so long for me to experience Italy. On prior trips to Europe as an architecture student at Carleton I had been to England, Scotland, Ireland, France, Spain, Switzerland, Germany and the Netherlands. I recall intentionally skipping past Italy, as I thought it would

---

1 Bente entrusted me to be the technical editor of the English edition.
2 *Vedute* are historic painted city scenes, often made as souvenirs of Grand Tours of Europe.

merit a special trip all to itself. So it was not until January 1984 that I finally set foot in the country. It was the beginning of a six-month sojourn studying at ICCROM, the International Centre for the Conservation and Restoration of Monuments, before embarking on travels throughout much of Italy to research the work of Carlo Scarpa. This started my fascination with the country, which has become perhaps my favourite place to visit.

In my late twenties I was chosen as the Canadian participant for the program sponsored by UNESCO (United Nations Educational, Scientific and Cultural Organization) at ICCROM's Via di S. Michele digs in Trastevere. Others in the program came from Brazil, Cuba, Denmark, England, France, Finland, India, Japan, Kenya, Poland and Spain.

The first task upon my arrival in Rome was to find a place to live, and the previous year's Canadian student had tipped me off to a cheap *pensione* in the *centro storico,* in an eighteenth-century building at Largo della Fontanella di Borghese. The lodgings were fashioned from a Renaissance building opposite the grand Palazzo Borghese at the far end of Via dei Condotti. Dingy and sad as the place was, it suited my budget and I had little choice but to accept it as my Roman home. To reach my tiny room with a sagging bed and little more than a sink, I had to navigate a long dark corridor and a tight spiral staircase. I used the grimy shared bathroom next door sparingly. Yet my room was brightened by a very large window with chestnut brown shutters that opened over the rooftops of Rome, with the dome of the Pantheon not far away.

What architect would not revel in a routine that meant seeing the Pantheon twice a day on the long walk to and from school? Each weekday started with a quick stop at the bar on the ground floor of the *pensione.* Breakfast, taken standing at the counter, consisted of cappuccino, a *cornetto* and a *sprumute di arancia.* Then there was a long walk through the narrow streets of the *centro storico,* through Piazza della Rotonda, then the Largo di Torre Argentina, through the Ghetto and the Portico d'Ottavia, across the Tiber to the Isola Tiberina in Trastevere, then on to ICCROM, which was housed in the vast Ospidale di San Michele building bordering the Tiber. I have traced that route on my copy of Giambattista Nolli's map of Rome, and very little has changed since it was engraved in 1748.

Every weekday our group of twenty met in a dark lecture room to view

slides and listen to lecturers from around the world talk about historic conservation. As an introductory exercise, each of us made a presentation about something they were doing in their home country. At the time, Vancouver was just shy of its centennial, so my presentation of its relatively young stock of heritage buildings was a contrast to the other more ancient global presentations. It did not take long for me to bond with Bente Lange from Denmark and Agnès Cailliau from France. We soon discovered we had a shared interest in the work of Carlo Scarpa, an architect now recognized for his genius in working distinctive modern interventions into historic buildings.

On the orientation day of our six-month course, we were treated to lunch at a typical Roman *trattoria*. There, we learned from the matronly school administrator some of the rules of dining in Italy. Rome is filled with such places where simple food, steeped in tradition, is served. Romans have a particular fondness for pastas *alla carbonara, cacio e pepe, alla vongole* or *amatricciana.* Other dishes, such as *saltimbocca, carcioffie alla guidecca* and *fritto misto,* are found in *osterie, ristorante* and *trattorie* ranging from rustic to elegant. The difference is in the presentation, the napery, the décor of the room and the price, but the food is reliably familiar. That's the way Romans like it.

At that first lunch we learned that bread is only eaten before the pasta course. I learned the hard way by having my hand slapped by the senora as I reached for another piece of bread just as the *spaghetti al pomodoro* arrived. I also learned that pasta is eaten with a fork and never a spoon, so I had to learn to twirl the strands adeptly. The fish or meat course is next, served plainly on the plate. Any vegetables, called *contorni,* often steamed spinach, are served in a separate dish on the side. Dessert is not very important in Rome, so it might be just fruit. And coffee at lunchtime is only espresso. Asking for a cappuccino or any other "milky coffee" after noon is frowned upon, as such beverages are reserved for infants, the elderly or the invalid. The rules are tricky, but once I learned them, they have stuck with me ever since. To this day I have narrowed down my coffee preferences to a short *macchiato* in the morning, an *espresso doppio* after lunch and maybe one in the late afternoon. Never a milky coffee in the afternoon.

Over the course of the next six months, I would enjoy many meals of delicious, simply prepared food, and memories of those meals are still vivid. When Bob Ledingham came to visit me at Easter that year, we stayed at the posh Hotel Inghilterra, next door to the Valentino shop and a block from the Spanish Steps. I never showed him the sad room I rented in the *pensione* at Largo della Fontanella di Borghese.

During that visit, we ate well. One memorable lunch was at Il Passetto, a very formal restaurant that dated from Rome's La Dolce Vita heyday of the 1960s. In the modernist wood-panelled dining room, we were served an elegant meal that started with a simple pasta course, then *branzino* cooked in parchment, followed by a single perfect orange. It was peeled in one impressive cut, tableside, by a handsome waiter who then arranged the segments in a circle on the plate, squeezing the juice from the membrane. That was it. Absolutely astonishing in its simplicity and memorable to this day.

I recall another meal at the very traditional *trattoria* La Matricianella, just steps from my *pensione*: a *frito misto* of sweetbreads and *cervello* (brains), veal *saltimbocca,* fresh spring asparagus as the *contorni* and then the tiniest and sweetest *fruiti di bosco* (strawberries) dressed *alla romana* with lemon and black pepper. That is how I always serve strawberries when they are in season.

But usually I would have a simple lunch with Bente and Agnès at an *osteria,* often at the Campo di Fiori, where we would sit in the square and watch the morning market being dismantled while we ate *bisi e pisi* and drank cheap *vino.* Evenings on my own would usually be spent at La Madelenna, then the cheapest decent *trattoria* near my digs, where dinner would consist of a dish of pasta, a *quartino* of *vino di casa* and a *mezzo* of *aqua minerale.* Occasionally I treated myself to a *gelato* at Giolliti, just a short walk away.

(•◆•)

Contrary to what I may have implied so far, spending six months in Italy meant more than just eating. My early friendship with Bente and Agnès, and our mutual interest in Scarpa, led to many excursions, both for research and to explore the country. Bente was staying at the Academia Danese in the Villa Borghese park, and I was often invited there for communal meals with her Danish colleagues. She also had access to an old car from the Academia and the use of a vintage set of Touring Club Italia guidebooks printed in 1928. Despite the modernization of the Italian highway system with *autostrade* in the ensuing decades, those guidebooks took us to places all over Lazio, Campania and the Veneto on well-travelled roads.

Agnès and her partner Paul Francois, a doctor, had come from Paris just two months after their son Côme (Cosimo in *italiano*) was born. They stayed in a vast flat belonging to Agnès's aunt that stretched across the east side of the Piazza Navona. Coincidently, it offered a direct view of Borromini's Sant'Agnese in Agone church. I was invited to spend many evenings there over dinner, and we used it as the meeting place for excursions around and out of Rome. Having a newborn in tow for visits to architectural landmarks opened many doors that were marked *chiusi per restauro* – Agnès and tiny Cosimo could charm any gatekeeper. How Agnès balanced caring for a baby with her studies at ICCROM was a mystery, but I was happy to pitch in whenever needed.

Agnès had friends at the French Academy in Rome, housed in the magnificent sixteenth-century Villa Medici, with its stuccoes by Michelangelo and modern interiors by Balthus. For the lavish masked ball of the Carnevale, which was held there annually, the villa was transformed into a discotheque and the garden lit for the evening with hundreds of tiny oil lamps lining the gravel paths. As many of the other academies in Rome were invited to the party, I was privileged to attend as a guest of the Danish contingent. They were all dressed in togas, while I made myself up as Dirk Bogarde playing Aschenbach in the film version of *Death in Venice*. My thinking was that as Carnevale was most closely associated with Venice, my costume should be too. It was all rather bacchanalian, with strobes lighting up the ancient walls of the salon. When Queen's "Radio Gaga" was spun on the turntable, the dance floor in the grand central salon was packed.

The party went on all night, and I vaguely recall a very drunken walk home down the Spanish Steps, along Via dei Condotti, and then collapsing in my sagging bed, fully dressed, with my slicked-and-dyed hair and rouged cheeks staining the pillow at my *pensione*.

As the course work at ICCROM carried on, it was apparent to us that there should be more to being in Rome than sitting in a dark classroom looking at slides. Bente was particularly impatient with the pace and dry content of the lectures we sat through, so we started playing hooky to explore Rome and planning trips farther afield.

In the company of Bente, Agnès, Paul and Côme, I travelled to Tivoli, Herculaneum and Pompeii; spent a weekend at the seaside in Sperlonga; explored Etruscan tombs and visited gardens at Bomarzo and the Villa Farnese; and eventually made it up to the Veneto.

(•◆•)

For our research project, the three of us decided to collaborate on a study of Carlo Scarpa's work at the Museo Castelvecchio. I had been fascinated by his work in Verona when I read of his interventions there in an architectural journal prior to leaving for Rome.[3] In the early 1980s, Scarpa's work dating from the 1950s and early 60s was still quite fresh and not as widely known and respected as is it today. His bold work, fastidious detailing, use of traditional materials in modern ways and keen eye for composition are still relevant to today's designers.

We planned a trip to Verona to meet with Arrigo Rudi, the architect who had worked with Scarpa on the museum, and Licisco Magagnato, its director. Making travel arrangements before the Internet and cell phones took some creativity and persistence – and luck. Bente was fluent in Italian, so she made the arrangements using the only phone available to students at ICCROM. While she was in the phone booth on the landing, speaking to the director about our pending visit, her conversation was overheard by another student, Biccha, who was waiting to use the phone. It happened that Biccha

---

3 "The Legendary Castle: Museo Castelvecchio, Verona", in a 1981 issue of *Progressive Architecture*, was the first I had heard of Scarpa.

had worked with Rudi and had a flat in Venice, and she offered it to us for our trip to the Veneto. That happenstance led to an incredible two weeks of travel and exploration in Verona, Vicenza, Treviso and finally Venice.

We took the train to Verona and stayed there for several days while we toured the *museo,* looked at drawings and met with Rudi and the museum director. The building is a vast assemblage of brick and stuccoed structures along the bend in the Adige River, including a bridge that spans the river,

in central Verona. Dating from the mid-fourteenth century, it was built as the home of the Della Scala family, then was used for centuries by the military, including as an arsenal and barracks during the Venetian period. Much of it was destroyed by Napoleonic forces at the end of the eighteenth century. Then it was rebuilt (by the French) then used by Austrian forces and later by the Italian military, until it became an art museum in 1924. Scarpa's radical rebuilding took place from 1958 to 1964; he used the building's history of additions, destruction and rebuilding in his approach to reimaging the museum's structure. He also oversaw the organization of the collections of sculpture and paintings, and designed a wall, pedestal, bracket or easel for each work of art.

We wanted to understand how Scarpa worked, how he decided to strip away parts of one end of the main wing to reveal the interior and expose his insertions of concrete beams and columns, timber framing and copper roofing. His signature move was to position the equestrian statue of Cangrande on a concrete beam, half under the roof and half outdoors, to mark the intersection of the key parts of the building's different eras of construction. Inside, he added Verona marble flooring with a slim border that was held back inches from the old walls. Archways in the rough stone walls were lined with slabs of creamy pink Verona stone, which he also used in a mosaic pattern of a square-within-a-larger square – an old Venetian motif – in the modern cladding of an entrance pavilion. New charred redwood window frames – *legno bruciato* – were mounted just inside the old gothic-arched stone openings, emphasizing a marked contrast between new and old. It was like a new lining inside an old shell.

Scarpa was a master with metalwork. Blackened steel straps were used to make sliding door panels. Bronze bars were fashioned into custom easels for medieval paintings and wooden religious panels. Large canvases were mounted on walls of *stucco lustro – or marmorino* polished Venetian plaster – deeply pigmented with colours that related to the paintings.

After Verona, we went on to see more of Scarpa's work in Venice. Biccha's flat was located in a garret not far from Piazza San Marco. It was the end of March, the weather was cool but bright, and the tourists had not yet descended. We toured Scarpa's art installations inside the Museo Correr and the jewel box of a showroom for the Olivetti typewriter company, which was then used as an art gallery,[4] with terrazzo floors, polished plaster, stone slab–covered doors and bronze detailing. Last on our itinerary was the astonishing work Scarpa had done at the Fondazione Querini Stampalia. From his graceful bridge across the canal, with the handrail

---

4 The Olivetti showroom has been restored as a museum and is run by FAI, Fondo Ambiente Italiano—"the National Trust for Italy" as it says on their website.

detailed in teak and bronze, to the steel gridded doors on the boat slip, one entered a series of spaces where his genius with materials and details flourished. As he had done in Verona, Scarpa added new stone floors with edging held back from the old brick walls by a slim gap. Polished plaster panels with custom metal light fixtures were used in the central gallery space, and in the garden there was an arrangement of paving stones, with steps, water channels and fountains, that showed exquisite detailing. The influence of Scarpa's work in that courtyard can be seen in a garden in Toronto by the Canadian architects Shim–Sutcliffe.

When Bente returned to Rome, Agnès and I decided to attend the opera at La Fenice. To dress for the occasion, I went shopping for a slim raw-silk tie in a dark bronze colour. From our seats high up in the gods, we watched Marilyn Horne and Samuel Ramey on stage in *L'Italiana in Algeri*. As we had not eaten in our dash to meet the curtain time, we needed to find a place for what Agnès called *le souper*, which I gather is a Parisian tradition, a light meal of soup and champagne after the opera. Venice is notorious for closing early, and finding a *ristorante* was a challenge. We finally followed a man with a flowing cape (who no doubt had also attended the performance at La Fenice) down many narrow winding and deserted *calle*, like something out of *Don't Look Now*. He led us to a lively restaurant hidden behind a dark facade, filled with opera-goers. And we did have soup, a Venetian fish version of *cioppino*, and a glass of *prosecco*.

(◦◆◦)

Although Scarpa was the focus of our sojourn, we could not miss the chance to tour the sixteenth-century works of the other celebrated architect from the Veneto, Andrea Palladio. His legacy, largely the result of his *Four Books on Architecture*, had an immense impact on the development of design in England (Christopher Wren, Inigo Jones and Colen Campbell) and America (Thomas Jefferson). Even in Ontario, his influence can be seen in the pedimented façades of Elgin County's courthouse and Ottawa's Rideau Hall.

Another ICCROM colleague, Jaakko Antti-Poika, an architect from Helsinki, joined Bente, Agnès and me for a Palladian weekend based in Vicenza. From our modest hotel we could see Palladio's Basilica, the massive city hall and market building dating from 1546 that faced the main piazza in the city. Its stacked arcades of Doric columns and arched openings showed his mastery of proportion and scale. After touring the remarkable interior of the Teatro Olimpico – with its stage set of exaggerated perspective – and the Villa Rotonda, we set out to see some of his villas in the countryside.

You will recall that Bente had access to a 1928 edition of the Touring Club Italia guidebooks, and we used the Veneto volume to navigate the

region around Vicenza in a tiny rented Fiat Panda. The opening hours had not changed in the five decades since the guidebook had been published, and we were lucky to choose the one day of the month – the first Saturday, I recall – when many of the villas were open. The one thing that had changed was the introduction of highways and *autostrade*. Nonetheless, we managed to follow the old roads to visit several Palladian villas that day, including the Villas Caldogno, di Maser, Emo and Cornaro. Our rental car got in a minor accident with a wedding party, but everyone involved just shrugged, and we all carried on our separate ways. Jaakko, our driver, was a bit shaken, and the four of us were exhausted by the day's outing, but thrilled to have been immersed in Palladiana.

(•♦•)

The handwritten report of our research was bound with sketches, plans and details which we submitted as our course assignment at the end of June. Then we made a presentation with slides to our class. It was quite a departure from the more traditional conservation studies others had presented, and some looked at our work with raised eyebrows.

Scarpa's work in Verona was just twenty years old at that time, so it was viewed with scepticism by pure conservationists. He had taken liberties with historic fabric and had a modernist eye for composition and detail. But in our view, he was showing how new and old can coexist, how new fabric can be compatible with yet distinguishable from historic fabric and still be a product of its time. That theme would be the topic of my master's thesis fourteen years later, when I wrote "Modernism in Context" at the University of York.

With the ICCROM course finished, I set off on a month of travel around Europe, beginning with a flight to Helsinki to spend a week with Jaakko and his family. The very long days of a Nordic summer meant plenty of time to tour the city and many of the works of Alvar Aalto. Then I went to Copenhagen for a week with Bente. Finally, I joined Agnès and her family at their summer home on the Côte d'Azur at le Cap Bénat.

(•◆•)

Since that extended time living in Rome, I have been back many times and have read up on its history in books such as Robert Hughes's *Rome* and Jake Morrissey's *The Genius in the Design*, where the rivalry of Bernini and Borromini is brought vividly to light. It's a story that is as worthy of a screenplay as the Mozart and Salieri rivalry that became *Amadeus*. I had a particular interest in Borromini after seeing his San Carlo alle Quattro Fontane and Sant'Agnese in Agone. Their baroque interiors are master-pieces of complex and fluid design. The lovely spiral spire of his Sant'Ivo alla Sapienza is perhaps the most delightful in Rome and was the inspiration for Vor Frelsers Kirke in Copenhagen, whose outside spiral steps, clad in copper, I have traversed several times. But I had never seen the interior of Sant'Ivo . . . until my sixtieth birthday.

I couldn't become a sexagenarian anywhere other than Rome. But as it was the year after Bob died, I did not want to go there alone. So I invited Bente and Agnès to join me along with four Canadian friends, including Neil Ironside, an old friend from Pentry Lane days, for a few days of cele-bration. We started my birthday with a tour of Rome, each of the seven in our group on the back of a Vespa with a traffic-savvy Roman driver. The itinerary was ours to choose, and with Bente's fluent Italian she talked us into the tiny, perfect Sant'Ivo church, perhaps Borromini's most remark-able achievement. It was astonishing to finally step inside this tiny church with its oval shape defined by convex and concave shapes masterfully inter-twined in the floor plan and ceiling design. Then our drivers conveyed us up to the Janicolo to see Bramante's Tempietto, also for the first time as on previous visits both buildings had always been *ciuso*.

We had a splendid alfresco lunch at Vecchia Roma of *linguine alle vongole*, and then toured the gardens of the Villa Medici. That night we met for *negronis* at my hotel bar, and for the first time I saw Bente in a dress, a simple, chic navy linen shift that was perfect with her cropped red hair. Then an alfresco dinner at my old haunt La Matricianella, just steps from Largo della Fontanella di Borghese.

(♦♦♦)

I have since taken other trips to Italy, organized around kayak adventures with Marco Venturini of TravelinKayak. With small groups I have toured the Marche, Umbria, the Dolomites and Lake Garda in Marco's capable hands, mixing paddling with historic sites, art and very good food, but the best trip was the first, when our group spent a week paddling the entire Venetian Lagoon. And that trip has a Scarpa connection.

The first two days we spent in the wilds of the eastern lagoon, enjoying the quiet solitude of the marshes and seabirds while navigating the channels marked with special oak poles called *briccole*. This was what the region must have looked like centuries ago, before the hordes of tourists and hulking cruise ships that have ruined Venice for many people. When we landed to stay overnight on Burano, we hauled up our kayaks at a slip in the central canal, causing quite a stir. The next day we aimed for Venice and paddled under bridges, past the Arsenale, attracting even more attention, then out across the Grand Canal to Isola San Giorgio, where we were staying in rooms at the Venetian Sailing Club. It was bliss to be in Venice for four days, but away from the packed *calle* and squares around Piazza San Marco and the Doge's Palace, which we could admire from a distance.

Each morning, we would take the *vaporetto* to a different neighbourhood, and Marco would lead a tour of the back streets and show us hidden places for *caffè* and lunches. We would nap for a bit back at the clubhouse, then in late afternoon, when kayakers were allowed to navigate the canals, Marco would lead us through the maze of waterways, away from the tourists. On more than one occasion, as our flotilla of five kayaks paddled along – again attracting attention – someone would yell "Ciao, Marco" from a bridge. He was clearly well known there, and knew the city well.

But there were some things he did not know, as I learned when I offered to take the group to see some of Carlo Scarpa's buildings one morning. The first stop was the Olivetti showroom in Piazza San Marco. Since the last time I had been there, it had been restored as a museum by the FAI. That day it was officially closed, but Marco charmed the docent into letting us in, and we had the place to ourselves. Scarpa's vision had been restored, as the place now had vintage Olivetti typewriters on display in the custom-made shelves and cases, and the terrazzo, polished plaster, marble and bronze detailing were still there.

Next I led the group to the Fondazione Querini Stampalia, where I pointed out Scarpa's genius of design and detailing. Marco was impressed, and he also appreciated the discovery, in one of the older galleries on the upper floor, of a small room entirely lined with framed *vedute* of Venetian life from the eighteenth century painted by Gabriel Bella. He studied every one of the sixty-seven scenes.

(• ♦ •)

Romans are noted for their love of pasta. In Rome there are the Famous Four: *cacio e pepe, alla gricia, alla carbonara* and *all'amatriciana*. But I think there is a fifth pasta that deserves noting – *Alfredo.*

Bob and I had the guilty pleasure of the signature *fettuccini* dish at Alfredo alla Scrofa, said to be the origin of that remarkably simply but much mangled pasta recipe. There are just three ingredients: butter, grated *Parmigiano* and *fettucine.* Never cream, shrimp, chicken tenders or even cracked pepper. It is prepared tableside by the waiter, who first melts the butter in a chafing dish, then slowly adds the grated cheese, carefully folding it in until it melts into a sauce. Then he twirls in the *fettuccini* (with a bit of pasta water trailing behind as a binder), all mixed with a grand display of bravado and served on a large oval platter. It is enough cholesterol for four, but the two of us ate every bite. Years later I would order it again and eat the entire serving alone. That afternoon I stumbled out onto Via della Scrofa in a happily sated stupor that lasted until the next day.

(◆)

TORDENSKJOLDSGADE

THERE ARE TWO watchtowers at either end of the Knippelsbro Bridge that have rounded ends and alternating bands of copper cladding with strip windows beneath projecting observation rooms. These are the lookouts for the bridge masters who control the lift bridge that opens Copenhagen's main havn (harbour) to the inner Islandsbrygge. The towers were designed by the architect Kay Gotlob in 1937, and their patinated copper panels echo the copper domes, spires and roofs of historic Copenhagen in a distinctly modern way.

I saw them on my first visit in 1984 and they fascinated me so much that I used them to illustrate my master's thesis "Modernism in Context" I wrote decades later. They show the way new and old can coincide in harmony and reflect the character of a place.

While I have never actually lived in Copenhagen, I have been there many times to visit Bente Lange, and I have a singular fondness for Denmark. It holds a special place as inspiration for my work with heritage buildings. My friendship with Bente began when we bonded in Rome in 1984 during our studies at ICCROM and developed through our shared interest in the work of Carlo Scarpa. The summer after my studies in Rome, I spent a week at Bente's flat in Christianshavn. We drank tea and ate stem ginger biscuits on the quay of the canal in front of her building, toured the

Danish countryside and stayed at her family's thatched summerhouse on the North Sea coast near Sjællands Odde, a short distance from the architect Arne Jacobsen's celebrated *røgeriet* (smokehouse). We cycled along the seashore and through gardens where ripe currants glistened ruby red in the summer sun. On subsequent visits she had moved to the sylvan suburbs of Copenhagen, and from there I explored much more of Denmark.

During the summer of 1998, while I was based in York writing my thesis, I was happy to escape the north of England to travel to Denmark for research. Of the sixty-eight buildings I visited and researched that summer, eleven were in Denmark, and I count Arne Jacobsen's sublime St. Catherine's College at Oxford as the twelfth Danish building, despite its being on British soil.

I admired how skilled Danish architects were at making modern buildings that respected their context, were simple but elegant and used traditional materials in spare and practical ways.

(•♦•)

In 2009 when I was competing in the Outgames, Bente gave Bob Ledingham and me the key to her flat at Tordenskjoldsgade in the centre of Copenhagen. The tongue-twisting street is named after Peter Jansen Wessel Tordenskjold, an eighteenth-century naval captain who is held in high esteem in Norway and Denmark, this despite his having lived only to the age of thirty. Located a half block from the harbour and about the same distance from Konigs Ny Torv square, Tordenskjoldsgade was lined with nineteenth-century buildings, mostly apartments six storeys high. It is also just a short bike ride to Havnebade (Harbour Baths) in the inner Islandsbrygge, where the swim part of the Outgames triathlon was held. One of the early works of BIG architects (the Bjark Ingels Group, whose cheeky website address is *big.dk)*, Havnbadden has a floating wooden deck – a big raft, moored to the quay – which frames the seventy-five metres length of swimming area. You are swimming in the harbour water, something the locals are quite proud of because of its cleanliness. It is free, too, and very popular during the short but bright Nordic summer.

Not far away on a canal that cuts through Christianshavn is another waterside delight, Bente's favourite summer restaurant, Christianshavns

Badudlejning & Café. This floating barge-cum-café is where Bente took us for an alfresco lunch just before she left for a country retreat. I was pleasantly surprised that my distaste for herring was dispelled when it was served in a curry sauce. I happily ate it while quaffing Tubourg and watching the parade of tour boats and watercraft pass by the café.

The day after our arrival was the half-marathon, something foolish to have entered as I was jet lagged and frustrated trying to re-assemble my bicycle which I had hauled along for the trip. But the running course was scenic and devoid of hills, and I recorded a decent time. To celebrate that night, we dined at Mielcke & Hurtigkarl, a restaurant on a list that foodie friends had given me, housed in an historic *orangerie* on the grounds of lush Frederiksberg Park. Four of us dined on course after course of artfully presented, witty and delicious food paired with excellent wines. The garden setting was gorgeous, and the interior walls had delicate floral frescoes. It was a very special first meal in Denmark.

That week Bob and I cycled around town, visiting museums and art galleries, then retreated to Bente's flat in the late afternoon for tea. Her place, on the top floor of a nineteenth-century apartment block, had high ceilings, chalky white plaster mouldings, huge casement windows (both an inner set and an outer set to cope with the damp Copenhagen winters) and bare wood floors. She had furnished it with a mix of antiques, modern ceramics and splendid light fixtures.

The penultimate day of our week was the triathlon. The harbour swim was bracing but was over quickly, and thankfully the forty-kilometre bike course around south Copenhagen was mostly flat. I flagged a bit during the final ten-kilometre run but ended up on the podium with a second-place medal for my age group.

After touring and partying in Copenhagen and before departing on a cruise around the Baltic, Bob and I treated Bente to dinner at NOMA, at what was then the most celebrated restaurant in the world. NOMA is short for NOrdic MAds (*mads* is food in Danish), and everything served had a wild, foraged or native provenance. It was located in a nineteenth-century warehouse on the harbourfront. The restaurant had heavy timber beams that had been whitewashed, and the Danish modern walnut chairs had sheepskin throws evoking a spare Nordic minimalism. The kitchen staff

of twenty-five laboured over every detail and made clever presentations of chicken skin "crackers", live shrimp and tiny flower pots with micro carrots set in "soil" made of charred nuts and grains. I have long since forgotten the staggering tab (and the 3 percent surcharge to cover the Visa commission) but it was worth every krone.

(•♦•)

Several times I have stayed with Bente at her home in Svaneke at the eastern end of the island of Bornholm. Known to Danes as "The Holiday Island", Bornholm is in the Baltic Sea, closer to Sweden than to Denmark. My first occasion to visit Bornholm was twenty years ago, for a cycle tour with my brother Paul, and getting there involved an overnight ferry from central Copenhagen to Rønne. Now it is just a short ride on a high-speed hydrofoil ferry from the Swedish coast, just across the Øresund Bridge from Copenhagen.

Once you arrive on Bornholm, traversing the island is a delight. It is a beautiful place, steeped in history, agriculture, fisheries and nature. Sheer

cliffs of red granite – the source of stone for many of Copenhagen's historic buildings – mark the north coast, while forests and farms are found in the central area, and sandy beaches line the south coast. The island is particularly noted for its twelfth-century round stone churches. The architect Kay Fisker,[1] a pioneer of Danish modernism, started his career designing stations for the rail line that stretched across the forty-kilometre width of the island in the early twentieth century. The rails are gone, replaced by

---

1 Fisker designed the Danish Academy in Rome's Villa Borghese Park, where Bente stayed while studying at ICCROM. She was tasked with its recent restoration, and I was happy to return there to see the careful restoration work that Bente directed.

bike paths, but the stations survive, some now private houses and one is an arts centre.

On two occasions I was there in late June, timed with the *Kildefest,* which is a kind of summer solstice-cum-spring-water festival. The night before the celebration, local children comb neighbours' gardens for fresh foliage and flowers (anything in bloom), and overnight they weave lavish garlands for the festivities the following day. Marching bands from schools all over Scandinavia make their way to Svaneke for the parade through the village and end up at a park where food stalls are set up with local specialties, including mini donuts. Later that night a second parade takes place, with village folk marching to the beach with torches held high. The torches are then used to light an enormous bonfire fed by twigs, branches and anything that needed to be cleared out of village gardens. Atop the bonfire is a rather pagan stick figure symbolizing the end of spring and the start of summer. Or at least that's what I understood from the translation from Danish to English.

Food figured prominently in my summer visits to Bornholm, and cycling along winding rural roads leads to many farm-gate sales of *nye kartofler* (new potatoes) and *jordbær* (strawberries).

The most fun on a recent visit was cycling to a rural butchery for a long-table farm meal on an evening close to the summer solstice. It featured locally caught roe deer and copious platters of fresh vegetables. At that meal I was seated next to a lovely woman who said she was an artist. Bornholm is filled with artists, glassblowers, textile weavers and ceramicists, but when I learned she had the tiny studio in Svaneke where I had previously admired the quirky ceramics in the window, I knew she was being too modest. Gitte Helle's work has an international reputation. She calls her studio Containerjuvelen, which roughly translates as garbage-bin-jeweller, and she collects old dishes, crockery, figurines and anything made of ceramics, dismantles them and reassembles them in what could be called a mash-up.

Days on Bornholm began with a walk across the granite rocks on the shore opposite Bente and her partner Margarite's house to have a dip in the sea. The Baltic is very, very cold, so bracing that it was just an in-out-dip, after which we wrapped in terry robes to return for coffee and a breakfast of rye bread and Havarti while sitting on a bench overlooking the sea. The rest of the day was spent biking or driving to see the sights.

(•♦•)

In 1998 I made two trips to Denmark while researching my thesis, parts of which are recounted in "Castle Howards End". One of the visits coincided with the book launch of a massive tome on the work of Arne Jacobsen, and Bente invited me to attend. The event was held in the vast lobby of the Bank of Denmark, which Jacobsen had designed. The book, which I now have in my library, weighs over three kilos and has 560 pages, all written in Danish. As Bente usually says when I ask what a certain word is in Danish, "Why bother, we're the only ones to speak the language!" It is astonishing that the tiny country of Denmark, with a population no larger than that of British Columbia (and a land area just about the size of Nova Scotia) has a publishing industry that can produce such a splendid book for the tiny number of Danish speakers around the world. Mind you, Denmark has also produced Bang and Olufsen, LEGO, Hans Christian Andersen, Bjark Ingels (of BIG fame) and Bjork. Sorry! Bjork is from Iceland, but you get the idea. Denmark is a country that punches well above its weight.

And whether in Copenhagen, Svaneke or Rome, the places associated with Bente Lange have been important influences in shaping the life of this Canadian architect.

(♦)

THE BARBER HOUSE

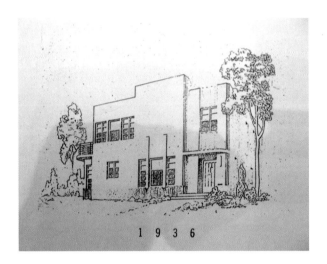

THE SUMMER PARTY was in full swing when I went down from the roof deck to check with June, the caterer. The kitchen was packed with guests, and as I talked to her I overheard a conversation between Guy, a fit young trainer from our gym, and Philip, a distinguished older man with silver hair, impeccably dressed. Philip had asked Guy how he knew Bob and me. Guy replied, "From the gym", and then he asked Philip what he did. Without a hint of importance, Philip simply said, "I'm the mayor". That Philip Owen, the mayor of Vancouver, and his wife, Brita, would grace one of our parties and add to the mix of friends, relatives, clients, artists and, yes, trainers, was one of the pleasures of living in the Barber House for almost three decades.

The story of the Barber House began on a dark and stormy night in 1988. It really was a dreadful late November evening with rain pelting down when Bob Ledingham and I first saw the inside of the house. The building was striking enough from the outside, being a rare Art Moderne house, cubic in shape and made of concrete, with a flat roof and unlike any of the other modest mid-1930s bungalows in Vancouver's West Point Grey neighbourhood. Located on the main bus route to UBC and set far back from the street on a doublewide lot, the house was a landmark. It was also one of the few "A" listed heritage houses on the city's west side, and was illustrated in *A History of Canadian Architecture.*

The city's heritage planner had phoned me earlier that very day to see if I could help rescue the house from demolition, a remarkable coincidence as we had already arranged our viewing. Bob and I had been looking to move from our rental apartment in Kerrisdale to something of our own. A deal to buy and rehabilitate a five-storey warehouse in Yaletown into lofts had fallen through just months earlier. Then we shifted our focus to look for something more like a townhouse. We did not want a typical house and yard. The Barber House seemed like a viable option, given its rather urban presence and its double lot.

By the time we finished our walk-through that November night, I had formulated an idea of how to restore the house (which had been split into two apartments) and build a second house in the rear yard to make use of density allowed on the double-lot site. We decided to make an offer that night.

It took the better part of eighteen months to work through the planning and approvals for the Barber House project, as the whole scheme was complicated by city zoning standards. We had to get special permission from the city council to build the rear yard infill house, the first of its kind in a single-family zone in the city. Some of the neighbours launched a campaign to oppose it, but we did finally prevail, and the project was completed in the summer of 1990.

The house is named after Horace Barber, a structural engineer who commissioned architect Ross Lort to create the design, though I have heard from Barber's descendants that Horace designed the house and Lort just drew it up. That rumour remains unsubstantiated.

The layout of the house was as unconventional as the structure and design. The main floor originally contained the entry hall, dining room,

kitchen, larder, furnace room and coal storage room. There was no basement. Upstairs was a spacious living room with corner windows affording
views out over the city, a den, three small bedrooms and just one bathroom.

Bob and I worked together on refining our idea for the renovation. We
would put the bedrooms on the main floor, leave the upstairs living room
as it was, and create a dining room and open kitchen from the warren of
small bedrooms. On the back, I designed a new exterior metal staircase to
lead up to a roof deck with splendid views of the city. The existing parapet,
visible from the street, worked perfectly as a balustrade for the new deck. A
large skylight was added to flood the kitchen with light as we did not want
to cut into the concrete walls with more windows.

The design inspiration was a modern version of what an Art Moderne
interior may have been like as we did not want to create a false museum
piece of the 1930s. We retained the original details of the second-floor
living room, including the stepped plaster ceiling and the metal-banded
concrete fireplace (although re-clad with black granite) with custom cast
iron fireplace dogs. During the renovations, we discovered that the house's
concrete exterior was supported on the inside by a frame of vertical steel
rails (actual railroad tracks) spaced four feet apart, with the space between
spanned by curved wooden slats, like barrel staves. That wooden cribbing

was the formwork for the poured concrete exterior shell. I was fascinated by this discovery and decided to expose it in the living room. A twelve-foot stretch of the wall was finished on the inside as three shallow curved recesses, lit from below. Bob designed a sofa to fit exactly below this feature.

We drew inspiration from the material palette of the work of Émile-Jacques Ruhlmann and Jean-Michel Frank and collaborated on a palette of exotic *avodire* wood with its zebra-like pattern, glossy porcelain floor tiles, *nero assoluto* granite countertops, automobile lacquer, *stucco lustro*, a wall of mirrors flanking the fireplace and tiny pale glass mosaic tiles. The colours were limited to amber, cream, charcoal and black, with aluminum leaf covering the walls and ceiling of the powder room, inspired by the Art Deco Savoy Theatre in London. Lutz Haufschild, a noted glass designer, created a set of three custom leaded glass windows for the stair hall and powder room. Bob's sofa was upholstered with a black patterned *gaufrage* fabric, and he commissioned gold silk cushions for it. The dining room featured a custom table with curved ends to echo the curves of the polished plaster dividing wall, and it was finished with a lacquered glaze over squares of taupe goatskin, with mother-of-pearl inlays.

(• ♦ •)

Bob and I were very proud of the Barber House and happy to show it off. For the housewarming, we hosted a party not unlike the one that the mayor attended. But on that hot August night it was a different crowd. The music had to be right, and for that I enlisted Clark Wilson,[1] one of the UBC architecture students I had hired that summer to do a heritage building survey, to create a playlist. The CDs he chose – B52s, Depeche Mode, ABBA, Liza Minnelli's *Results* and Madonna's *Immaculate Collection* – captured the musical taste of that summer. The party spread all over the house, but it was focussed mostly on the roof deck, with Clark holding court in his leopard-print suit.

Bob and I would time our parties for when June O'Connor was available. Guests would often inquire, when RSVPing, if she would be doing

---

1 I was Clark's thesis advisor for his UBC dissertation, "Gloria Swanson and the Phenomenology of Stairs". After UBC he studied landscape architecture at UC Berkeley. He now works for the Environmental Protection Agency in Washington DC. I am proud to see how his career has evolved.

the food. Her mushroom logs were famous, as was her wild boar pate, served on homemade baguettes. The Christmas parties had themes: variously, "Venetian Splendour", "Turkish Delight", or "Nordic Lights". After the miserable news of the financial collapse in the fall of 2008, we sent out invites for our holiday party saying just "Cheer Up, It's Xmas". People still talk about the upside-down Christmas tree, covered in white feathers, which had been inspired by Jean-Paul Riopelle's paintings of white birds that had graced the Canada Post stamps one holiday season. Of the one hundred or so invitations we sent out, the acceptance rate was usually in the eighty or so range.

We entertained often and hosted fundraising dinners for various arts and heritage charities. We had collected several sets of old china: a German Art Deco set, some Limoges from Bob's mother, and a set of 104 pieces of English Cauldon porcelain that we found in an antique shop on Pimlico Road in London, with thirty-six dinner plates and eighteen soup plates, plus platters, covered vegetable dishes and a beautiful large soup tureen. The broken lid of one of the vegetable dishes had been carefully repaired with a bronze wire staple. I loved the fact that the repair was visible, and I have used that lid in lectures to demonstrate a visible repair, not dissimilar to the painting *lacunae* technique I witnessed in the conservation lab at Le Louvre. We used those dishes with a vintage set of Art Deco Belgian silverware laid on Bob's goatskin dining table and always had beautiful flowers, often just tulips, Bob's favourite.

My interest in food was developed after I took a series of cooking classes at Dubrulle, a local culinary school. Margaret Chisholm was the instructor, and she was truly an inspiration. On several evenings over a six-week period we learned knife skills, stocks and sauces, pastry and pasta, breads, fish, shellfish, how to debone a duck and various ways of cooking vegetables. It was very much a hands-on program, and I learned from her the importance of *mise en place* and that cooking was every bit as much about preparation and temperature control as the actual cooking of the dish.

Several of our charity meals were prepared by chef Michel Jacob, the owner of Le Crocodile, Vancouver's finest French restaurant. Michel and an assistant would arrive with all the provisions for a multi-course meal to be served by Bob and me. On one occasion the dinner was for a group of ten well-heeled strangers who had purchased the dinner at a charity auction. The group arrived on a hot Sunday night in early July in a white stretch limousine. The men were casually dressed as if they had just come from the eighteenth hole at the golf course. Some of the women wore fuzzy sweaters appliqued with shimmery animal motifs. The menu had been specially designed and handwritten by Michel to accommodate one vegetarian, someone who did not eat red meat, and a celiac sufferer. This is what was served:

> *Magret d'Oie Fume au Porto Salade d'Haricot Vert*
> *Gateau au Crabe Sauce Verte Julienne de Poireaux Frits*
> *Soupe Froide au Champagne et Bettraves Rôties*
> *Filet de Loup de Mer Poëllé Sauce au Persil Chinois*
> *Chèvre Chaud et Salade Frisée Vinaigrette au Balsamic*
> *Framboises et Fraises au Cointreau Sorbet à l'Ananas*

Serving the splendid meal was complicated by the fact that between each course the guests changed places, so tracking the celiac sufferer and the vegetarian was challenging. But the best part was hanging out with Michel in the kitchen for our own private dinner party – Michel had brought extra of everything for us to enjoy.

A few years later, Michel invited me to work for an evening in the kitchen of Le Crocodile. Dressed in a white jacket, I was assigned to the cold station, helping to plate the salads and desserts. His kitchen ran quietly, like clockwork, with each of the seven members of the *brigade* being assigned a specific duty. Michel oversaw everything, as he had done since the late 1970s when he opened Le Crocodile, named after a celebrated restaurant in his native Strasbourg. There was no shouting or shaming, but Michel had a watchful eye on everything that was sent to the dining room. Anything that was not perfect had to be redone, from scratch, and then inspected again. My salads had to be plated exactly the same way every time, as there was no tolerance for culinary expression or spontaneity. I admire his approach to this day.

Most of the meals we enjoyed at the Barber House were not quite so elaborate, although we did on occasion host friends and family in the dining room. I enjoyed doing the cooking, while Bob was excellent at ironing the napery, serving as bartender and cleaning up. Eight at table was optimal, but there were occasionally ten. Mostly I made all the food, but sometimes I had help in the kitchen with plating and serving, filling wine and water glasses, and cleaning up. We tried our best to keep it simple, but inevitably things would get more elaborate and the dishes would pile up. There were times, having worked all day in the kitchen preparing the meal, when I wished that as the guests arrived I could sneak downstairs to the bedroom for a nap.

Our "kitchen suppers" were much more intimate and enjoyable. There was an upholstered banquette built into the end of the kitchen – I like to incorporate a banquette when I design a kitchen – with a round table and two chairs. It was perfect for four, and that is where we shared meals with our closest friends. We would host these often on a Friday or Sunday night, with scant notice, if we were not spending the weekend at Estergreen.

My collection of cookbooks was housed in the bookcases flanking the banquette and included signed copies of books by the chefs of many of the celebrated restaurants where we had dined: Bishop's, Charlie Trotter's, Daniel, The French Laundry, Jean-George, Mugaritz, NOMA, NOPI, The River Café, Rockpool, Scholteshof, St. John and Willow's Inn were all represented. All but The River Café are helmed by men, but the books that I actually cooked from were almost all by women: Alison, Claire, Claudia, Fanny, Irma, Julia, Marcella, Martha, Nigella, Patricia and especially Elizabeth.

Elizabeth is the ground-breaking cookery author Elizabeth David. I first heard of her from an article titled "Elizabeth the First" in the *Independent on Sunday* when I was in Dorset a few years after she died. I was fascinated that her writing was not just recipes but also about food, meals and her travels and living in Italy, Egypt and France. I turn to her books frequently, not just for recipes (her *gateaux au chocolat* is a mastery of terse perfection) but equally for the stories about food. She wrote about a visit in 1958 to Chez Barattéro, a celebrated restaurant in Lamastre, in her book *An Omelette and a Glass of Wine*. I read about it years after Bob and I had gone on a tour of the Rhône valley and headed up to Lamastre in the Ardèche region to dine, unknowingly, at the same restaurant she had. Dining at

Chez Barattéro we had the same *poularde en vessie* (chicken poached in a pig's bladder) served at the table that Elizabeth David wrote about. Pale and succulent, it was delicious.

My interest in food, of course, aligns with my interest in kitchen design. Most of my architectural commissions began with the design or redesign of kitchens. At the Barber House, I laid out the design in the space of what had been two small bedrooms with two small windows in the concrete outer walls. The long narrow space had an L-shaped counter along the east and south walls, with the main sink under the east window and a gas cooktop and double wall ovens next to a hulking Traulsen refrigerator. The long island had a prep sink and an appliance garage to shield the kitchen mess from the open-plan living areas. The cabinets were finished with high-gloss automobile lacquer, the island millwork was clad in *avodire* wood to match that in the rest of the house, and there were black granite countertops with a reverse bevel edge. The backsplashes were clad in off-white Corian to match the other painted walls. The closets that divided the kitchen from the dining room were finished with glossy *stucco lustro* pale cream tinted polished plaster. The pivoting door panel to the dining room was made of *avodire* with a special profile shaped like an airplane wing in plan, to mimic the opposing curve of the polished plaster wall. Mounted high on that wall was a row of six ceramic pears, echoing a large painting of pears by William Roberts that hung over the banquette and an old pear tree that grew just outside the kitchen window. French doors squeezed into the width of the one old window frame led to the metal landing and the stairs to the roof deck.

(•♦•)

Of all the kitchens I have designed for friends and clients, Mamie Angus's stands out. She and her late husband bravely gave me free rein on a layout inspired by the pantry in Edwin Lutyens' Castle Drogo, a place I had admired on my British Council-sponsored tour in 1980. Mamie had a large breakfront, twelve feet long, that had once been installed in a shop in Provence. To incorporate that piece, I proposed an "unfitted" kitchen, arranged in a perfectly square room with furniture pieces instead of conventional cabinetry. In a nod to Castle Drogo, I designed a circular central island, seven feet in diameter, in the centre of the room. The island housed two sinks and the dishwasher. An antique French crystal chandelier was hung within an oculus above the island. On the west wall were a fireplace and doors to the terrace. On the south wall was a box-bay window with an antique settee and dining table. On the blank east wall stretched the antique cabinet. The gas range was on the north wall, with doors to the dining room and pantry. There was no refrigerator in the kitchen, as Mamie was happy to have it out of sight in the pantry.

Mamie invited Bob and me for Thanksgiving dinner shortly after the kitchen was finished. The layout was put to the test with Mamie, Bob and me stationed around the perimeter of the island, trussing the bird, chopping the vegetables, spinning the salad greens or ricing the potatoes, while other guests chatted and sipped *chablis* while watching from the settee or standing by the roaring fire.

(• ◆ •)

In 2006 we thought it might be time to leave the Barber House, as we had purchased a pre-sale at Jameson House, a downtown high-rise project that I worked on with Foster + Partners. We kept our options open by not selling the Barber House until we had tried condominium living, using the time while the house was vacant to have all the millwork refinished, the carpet replaced and the whole place painted inside and out. We refreshed the kitchen and installed new appliances. A gas range replaced the cook-top, and the double wall ovens were replaced by a steam/convection oven and a wine fridge. The Traulsen was replaced with a more practical (and quieter) refrigerator. There was no need for a microwave as I never had use for one.

But Bob's diminishing health changed our plans. We decided to sell the condo, accepting the one and only offer we received, and returned to the Barber House in April 2013. With his ALS diagnosis, Bob decided to close his office at 125 East 4th Avenue.

On the morning of May 2, I awoke to the sound of the front door shutting. As usual, Bob had gotten up first to fetch the newspapers and then head upstairs to the kitchen to make coffee and squeeze juices, orange for him and grapefruit for me.

Then I heard a dull thud and rushed to the hallway, where I saw Bob lying on the landing of the staircase, ramrod straight with his arms at his sides. I called 911. The newspapers were on the floor at the top of the stairs. Had he tripped on the top step due to his weak left leg? If so, wouldn't he have fallen forward and tried to break the fall with his arms? There was no sign of a stumble. Instead, he had fallen straight backwards to the landing halfway down. It seemed most likely he had had a stroke at the top of the stairs, dropped the newspaper, then fallen backwards. What triggered his fall would trouble me for a long time after that day.

Bob was dazed but speaking when the paramedics arrived. They eased him onto a stretcher, being careful of his head, and then into the ambulance. We drove without haste or sirens to Vancouver General Hospital, unaware of how badly his brain had been damaged. In the ER he was coherent; he knew he was at VGH and could name the prime minister.

Mid-morning, while I was standing in line for a coffee, I received a call that Bob's condition had worsened. On my return to the ER, I found a triage unfolding with a team of doctors swarming around him. His CT scan showed a massive haemorrhage in his brain; there was only a slim possibility of survival if heroic interventions were ordered. I was told that if he survived, he would likely be a vegetable. Having seen the misery his mother suffered for eighteen months after a post-stroke intervention, I decided to let him be. He was wheeled to a quiet room, where kind nurses administered hourly shots of morphine. We waited out the day. Bob was dead by six o'clock that night. I had lost my life partner just nine days shy of our thirty-second anniversary.

(• ◆ •)

For six more years I lived on alone at the Barber House. I even allowed the Vancouver Heritage Foundation to include it on their annual tour of heritage houses, something Bob would never have permitted. During the tour I stood at the kitchen sink to watch and listen as the parade of twelve hundred people wandered through the house. Most did not know that the modern-looking interior design was almost thirty years old. Corian wall panels in the kitchen? Polished plaster walls in the dining room? Zebra-striped wood panelling? Automobile lacquer on the kitchen cabinets? Aluminum leaf on the powder room walls? All of it looked fresh, and, a much overused term for the work of Robert Ledingham, timeless. No wonder he had received an honorary degree from his alma mater, the University of Manitoba. But I found the house rather lonely and quiet. The memories of living there for almost three decades were profound. I could never climb the stairs without pausing on the landing where Bob lay the day he died.

I contemplated moving to someplace smaller, as long as it had a decent terrace. One day the realtor who sold our Jameson House condo called me with news that he had just received a listing in Modena, a twenty-year-old building a short walk from the Granville Island public market. It was a generous sixteen-hundred square feet and had a vast terrace, almost as large as the suite. The interior was dated but the layout had potential for a major overhaul. The offer I made the next day was accepted later the same week. I was about to embark on a very satisfying project for a place of my own.

Then I had to sell the Barber House, something that took the better part of two years and three real estate agents. I later learned that the new owners had been amongst the crowd that had come through during the open house years earlier. Happily for me, they wanted not just the house but almost all the furnishings, including the custom sofa, goatskin dining table (and ten chairs), beds and some of the art original to our design.

I do miss living at the Barber House, but like many who have lived in historic buildings, it seemed like a period of extended custodianship. The house has been restored and designated as a heritage building and has a bronze plaque to show for it. The Barber House cannot be torn down.

Every now and then I drive by the house and am delighted to see it sitting on the sloped lawn framed by towering clipped cedar hedges that Bill Reed specified. On two occasions those hedges have attracted the attention of renowned architects and landscape architects.

(•♦•)

The real estate agent who showed us the Barber House on that dreadful November night was Penny Graham. She seemed to know everyone in Vancouver, who was upsizing or downsizing, getting divorced and in need of new digs. Penny Graham (née Sutherland) and her second husband Marty Zlotnik became very good friends. Penny often accompanied Bob and me for whirlwind theatre trips to Stratford. When Marty arranged a surprise church wedding for her on their 25th anniversary, we were honoured to be ushers. She often invited us for Sunday suppers of leftovers, but also to proper dinner parties. She made the best lemon curd tarts.

Penny kept the surname of her first husband David (they commissioned the Graham House in West Vancouver, one of Arthur Erickson's most notable buildings, now sadly demolished) and kept close to many of his family after their divorce. Because of her, a long list of Grahams - Andrew, Connie, Christopher, David, Helen, John, Jonathan, Sally and Sarah - filled the "G" page of our address book at Barber House. Various Grahams have kept me busy helping them with their houses in Vancouver, Hardy Island, Langley, Calgary, Sun Valley and The Desert.

Franco and I visit Penny at the hospital where she has been since Lewy Body Dementia has taken her speech, mobility and vitality. She had a glimmer of recognition when I showed her a photo from the last time we were in Stratford together. She is always beautifully coiffed and smartly dressed and seems to enjoy the lemon tarts we bring for her.

125 EAST 4TH AVENUE

W E ALL KNEW that McBeth was under the table as I was showing Herb and Diane the model of the house I was designing for them. What I did not know was that Diane had kicked off her shoes. It was only when she looked down to put them back on that she noticed little bits of tan leather scattered on the carpet. McBeth had been quietly and methodically nibbling at the leather of her Bally pumps. Deeply embarrassed, I offered right away to have them repaired, but Diane snapped that she needed them to get home. Of course. A gift certificate for replacement shoes and a lavish bouquet from the best florist in town were sent to her the next day.

Our Scottish terrier McBeth was a constant presence at the office I shared for many years with Bob Ledingham. She came to work every day and was much loved by staff, clients and delivery people. The postman often carried McBeth in his mailbag up the stairs to the reception desk. She had been a daily companion at Bob's previous office in Kitsilano, an old warehouse building he had converted to his interior design studio. Now, with more work and larger staff, he needed a bigger building, which he found in an industrial area in East Vancouver, just off Main Street. It had been a warehouse and chemical testing lab, with blast-proof glass on some of the windows and a mysterious concrete-block bunker in the rear.

Despite its unremarkable appearance, mismatched floor levels and slightly out-of-the way location, it had many positive attributes, such as ample floor space, a proper loading dock in the rear and an entire adjacent lot for parking. It was also reasonably priced at the time. The sign for Robert M. Ledingham Inc.[1] and Robert G. Lemon Architecture & Preservation went up at 125 East 4th Avenue in 1988.

Bob knew that I was good at space planning, so he asked me to plan the renovation of the building. I actually enjoy the constraints of working with existing conditions. The west part of the building, with two storeys and a partial basement, was adjoined to another two-storey section that had been built at a later time. Working with the old demarcations of the building, I came up with a plan for the main floor that had a lobby with stairs up to the reception area and design studio, two rental spaces and a warehouse space linked to the loading dock.

The upstairs was divided into three parts. First a reception area with granite floor tiles, lined with glass block and lacquered wall panels. Then down two steps to the studio space which extended the depth of the building. The existing bands of windows at both ends were supplemented by two large skylights I designed to be centred on the passageways that separated the fourteen workstations. The easternmost section had two spacious sample rooms, one for fabrics and leathers, the other for tiles, stone, wood and carpet. Our landscape architect friend Bill Reed enclosed the parking lot with tall, sharply pruned dense cedar hedges. The side of the concrete block building was covered by an old Boston ivy vine whose leaves turned stunning red and gold in the fall. A koi pond and bamboo thicket were added to the entryway, a nod to Bob's interest in Oriental design.

My architectural practice occupied two of the workstations, and it is from there that I ran my consultancy of both heritage conservation and

---

1 The name of Bob's firm would later be changed to Ledingham Design Consultants or LDC.

custom residential design, working on projects such as the house I was designing for Diane and Herb. When Bob and I had purchased the Barber House, its renovations kept my draftsman and me busy for eighteen months. Bob and I would often collaborate on each other's projects. When presented with a condominium floor plan that needed to be improved, Bob would usually ask me to do a layout, while grumbling about the poor planning of the building by the original architect. It was a puzzle to figure out how to get the bones right for Bob's interior design interventions. Only when the architecture was right would he begin his work. His forte was clearly design and not decorating. Many prominent architects would include Bob on their teams to make sure the integration of structure and interiors was seamless.

We worked together on a sprawling Shingle Style house on the West Vancouver waterfront that was a complete work of architecture and interiors. Bill Reed was part of the team from the inception so the landscape design was also fully integrated, from the siting of the house to take advantage of waterfront views to the detailing of brick pavers that were used on the terraces and around the indoor pool deck.

The architectural side of my practice yielded a range of projects from modest additions or renovations to heritage houses. There was extensive

work on a large Tudor Revival house in Shaughnessy that had belonged to my friend Connie Graham and her late husband, John. More contemporary in design was a row of three waterfront villas on tony Point Grey Road. Bob had invested in the Point Grey project and for a time owned one of the houses. The pity was that he sold the house for what seemed like a decent price. Waterfront property in Vancouver is rare, and that same house three decades later is worth twelve times the price he sold it for.

(•♦•)

In the late 1980s I was busy with heritage consulting work. I co-authored the amendments to the British Columbia Building Code for heritage buildings, which included a range of compliance alternatives to aid in upgrading existing conditions that did not meet the letter of the codes for new buildings. I also prepared rehabilitation guidelines for heritage buildings for both the City of Vancouver and the province of British Columbia. Because of my experience with guidelines I was invited to be part of the working party for the federal *Standards and Guidelines for the Conservation of Historic Places in Canada* when it was published in 2002.

I sat on the city's heritage advisory committee and chaired the design review committee, where we reviewed submissions for permits for heritage buildings. It was there that I observed the difficulties architects encountered when they were tasked with blending new and old buildings without creating pastiches. *That could be a topic for a future master's thesis,* I mused. Meanwhile, my own work amassed a large number of heritage awards.

My heritage building projects included a new cornice and a survey of the old wooden windows at Kensington Place, a prominent Spanish Baroque Revival apartment building overlooking English Bay. I worked on integrating the façade of the Palms Hotel into a theatre complex in downtown Vancouver. The storefront had been so badly renovated over the years that I got to design a new set of faux cast iron columns with faux palm leaf capitals as a nod to the historic design. I consulted on the rehabilitation of the Old Territorial Administration Building, an impressive wood frame building in the historic gold rush town of Dawson City, Yukon.

Feasibility studies and documentation of heritage buildings included the Kamloops Indian Residential School (now sadly in the news with the discovery of hundreds of unmarked graves of schoolchildren), St. George's School (a granite and terra cotta former convent), the Britannia Shipyard in Steveston and many buildings at the Barkerville Historic Site in B.C.'s Cariboo region. I prepared design guidelines for historic areas in Lower Lonsdale (North Vancouver), Kitsilano and the First Shaughnessy area (Vancouver). The Historic Style Manual I prepared for Shaughnessy is still referenced by the city's heritage program. The City of Vancouver commissioned me to study the potential designation of three downtown sites, one of which, Jameson House, I would later work on with Foster + Partners.

One commission that spanned residential design and heritage conservation was a project for Janet Campbell, whose kitchen I had redesigned in Vancouver. She had purchased the timber frame of an eighteenth-century house from Nova Scotia, to be re-erected on a remote site on Hernando Island off B.C.'s west coast. Hernando is a private island that is only accessible by water taxi. It is, for the most part, off the grid, with power supplied by the sun, propane, kerosene lamps and a backup generator. I visited the site for the first time with Janet in the dark days of winter. Foul weather meant the boat voyage from Lund to Hernando was in complete fog, but she had brought a picnic lunch, including a thermos of warm, homemade warm *vichyssoise*. After we landed, we traversed the building site along the waterfront and agreed on the location for the house, facing south and right beside a meadow.

Photos of the house prior to disassembly showed its simple shape, a storey-and-a-half high, with a central brick chimney, a symmetrical façade with a central front door and flanking mullioned windows. With just the house's timber frame to work with, I had to reimagine how its exterior doors, windows and cladding would be designed. I suggested that the historic front door location would be a "ghost door", much like the Ontario Gothic farmhouse I had designed at Carleton, with the real entrance located along a back porch that led to the kitchen. Janet was a superb cook, and the kitchen formed the centre of the house, anchored by a hefty fire-engine-red AGA range (adapted for propane), backed onto a massive central chimney. The rest of the house was meticulously finished, with the historic oak framing exposed and complemented by wood panelling, painted in what we felt were appropriate colours suitable to an east coast maritime saltbox, albeit reimagined on the west coast. The story of the project, "Coast to Coast", graced the cover of *Western Living* magazine in 1995.

She also commissioned me to rehabilitate a grand heritage house near Vancouver's city hall. It had a broad front porch and corner turret tower and was clad in very unusual glazed terra cotta blocks. She let me design a modern addition to the side and rear, detailed in a bronze and glass wrapped addition. I was able to put into practice some of what I had learned from my thesis, "Modernism in Context", about mixing old and new building components in compatible but distinguishable ways.

However, in 1991, after finishing with the Hernando Island project, my practice was put on hold while I took on the job of Senior Heritage Planner for the City of Vancouver, a post I held for five and a half years. My work there is described in "Twelfth and Cambie".

(• ♦ •)

Five years later, in the fall of 1996, when I was about to tender my resigna-
tion from city hall, I got a call from Peter Busby, one of Canada's prominent
architects who focussed on sustainability. He asked me to join his team
for a proposal to establish new headquarters for the Architectural Institute
of BC in an historic building in downtown Vancouver's Victory Square
area. For two years I worked out of his Yaletown office while continuing to
maintain my 125 East 4th Avenue shingle. The resulting project integrated
many elements of contemporary design and building practice with good
conservation measures. It was the beginning of many collaborations with
Peter's firm, which later became Perkins & Will.

When I was asked to rehabilitate the heritage First Church of Christ
Scientist in Vancouver for the Coastal Church congregation, I engaged the
team at Perkins & Will for the project. We used Corten (self-weathering)
steel for external seismic braces and for the distinctive cross.

Some of my other collaborations as consulting heritage architect with
established architectural firms were with Walter Francl on the Shaughnessy
Mansions renovation; the Wing Sang building, the oldest building in
Chinatown; and Jameson House (Walter's firm was the associated firm
with Foster + Partners). I also worked closely with MCMP Architects on the
conservation of a fascinating neo-Egyptian Art Deco terra cotta façade on
Granville Street, and then the façade of the former Quadra Club that was
incorporated into Kohn Peterson Fox's MNP Tower next to the landmark
Art Deco Marine Building.

One of the most fulfilling projects of my career was the rehabilitation
of the Hotel Georgia, a late-1920s neo-Georgian building in downtown
Vancouver, with Endall Elliot Architects. I advised on the conservation of
the brick and cast-stone exterior but also, more importantly, on the impressive range of interiors, many of them designated as heritage spaces. The
lobby had mahogany panelling that had to be documented and then partly
removed to allow seismic upgrading of the concrete support columns. The
elevator shafts were rebuilt as seismic buttresses, and the beautiful curved
terrazzo staircase was kept intact while a new shear wall was installed on
the other side. Most impressive was the Spanish Ballroom. To accommodate a new underground parkade, the entire ballroom was documented,
with detailed photos and sample casts of the elaborate plaster mouldings

that had survived. Then the ballroom was dismantled and, once the park-ade was completed, reconstructed, this time restored to its 1929 elegance. There had been many photos taken of the room in its early days, but over time the Spanish motifs of caryatids and garlands, all rendered in plaster, had been removed. Working with craftsmen at Ital Decor, we were able to restore the original decorations. The historic sheen on the plaster walls seen in the old photos was replicated using *stucco lustro,* a technique I had first seen at Carlo Scarpa's Museo Castelvecchio.

(•♦•)

Another significant project in my career was the rehabilitation of the Shannon Estate with Perkins & Will. Fans of *Carnal Knowledge* may recog-nize the Shannon mansion that was used as a set for the film, and the exterior is recognizable as the stand-in for the Cabot Mansion in *Best in Show.* The property was envisioned in 1912 by sugar baron B.T. Rogers as an idealized English country estate transported to south Vancouver. The four-hectare sloped site was situated on what had been Shannon's dairy farm, carved out of the wilderness. The gatehouse and perimeter wall were built first, then the

garage and stables. The Beaux Art mansion took a decade to complete, but Rogers was such a keen gardener that the sunken Italian and rose gardens were in bloom long before the mansion was habitable. By the time I started working on the project, the estate had changed hands twice, a townhouse development designed by Arthur Erickson's firm had been added to the grounds in the 1970s, and the heritage buildings had been sadly neglected. Clinging ivy and a massive wisteria vine had damaged the brick and cast concrete masonry, and the buildings were in need of seismic upgrading. Most of the principal rooms of the mansion were intact, although stripped of their original mid-1920s wallpapers and light fixtures.

My task as part of the massive site redevelopment – probably the most extensive conservation project of buildings, gardens and interiors in Vancouver – was to oversee conservation of the gatehouse, garage and stable buildings, mansion, perimeter wall and gardens. With the capable assistance of Ivonne Voelkel as my project heritage expert, our "conservation plan" was prepared, which spread to 264 large pages, detailing the history, condition and conservation treatment of each element.

The restoration of the interiors of the mansion was perhaps the most rewarding part of the project. The principal rooms had finally been

completed in 1925 by Mrs. Rogers, years after her husband had died – sadly, B.T. Rogers never saw the house completed. She hired a firm from New York for the interior decoration of the impressive main floor rooms: a full-length entry gallery with grand stair hall, a massive great hall with baronial fireplace, an elegant drawing room originally used as a music room, a wood-panelled dining room and a glazed conservatory. Most of the original wall coverings and light fixtures had been removed, but the panelling and plasterwork were intact, including traces of the historic wall, ceiling and trim colours.

We had access to a collection of photos taken in 1930, which gave evidence of the original wallpapers and light fixtures. One of the photos showed the elegant drawing room with crystal chandeliers and a grand Bösendorfer piano being played by Jan Cherniavsky, Mrs. Rogers' son-in-law. The missing light fixtures were reproduced by a firm in Toronto. For the replication of the wallpapers, I turned to Laura McCoy, an expert in New York, who worked from the photos to produce accurately scaled designs of the wallpapers in the great hall and drawing room. Of course, the black-and-white photos did not give any clues regarding colour, but Laura knew from experience what they could have been and consulted the

Smithsonian's historic wallpaper collection, held at the Cooper Hewitt Museum in New York, to determine the decoration tastes of the affluent in 1925. When the strike-off samples came, I was stunned by the boldness of the colours. The large-scale neo-Renaissance pattern had rich colours – deep and pale green, salmon and burgundy with shots of gold leaf. The sample was tacked up on the wall of the great hall and I awaited the verdict from the owner. He loved it. The more modest cream tones with a slight shimmering glaze also got his nod for the elegant drawing room.

To celebrate the fortieth anniversary of my architectural practice in the fall of 2019, I hosted a reception in the mansion's restored rooms. Rain dampened the garden party, but seventy-five guests mingled in the great hall over cocktails and canapés. Then I opened the sliding doors to the drawing room, where the guests were treated to a recital by the young Genesis Trio. It was wonderful to be in that room, filled with people seated on gilded chairs, the new wallpaper shimmering in the light from the replicated crystal chandeliers and hearing music much as it might have sounded in 1930.

(◆◆◆)

The final years of 125 East 4th Avenue are rather sad. Bob had planned to wind down his practice as he approached his seventieth birthday, and we intended to spend more time at Estergreen. He was having trouble walking, with signs of drop-foot, and was told that surgery to fuse the L4 and L5 vertebrae in his spine would fix those issues, but alas it did not. His walking was laboured, and he fell down on more than one occasion, once with a nasty gash to his skull.

Bob carried on at work and kept his staff of twelve busy, but he needed help navigating the stairs, and his receptionist would fetch his lunch from the deli down the street. Other staff took turns walking Ginger, our new Scottie, who came to work every day just as McBeth had done years earlier.[2] One night at a public hearing at city hall, where Bob had spoken in opposition to a rezoning proposal for a massive office tower just twenty-eight feet from our bedroom window at Jameson House, he collapsed on the floor of the council chambers as his left leg buckled under him. He was not hurt physically, but he was deeply embarrassed and bruised emotionally. That night I vowed to ramp up our investigation into his condition.

After many consultations with neurologists and specialists, and more frequent visits to physiotherapists, we heard for the first time about ALS. Amyotrophic lateral sclerosis (Lou Gehrig's disease) is an incurable, debilitating form of polyneuropathy. In layman's terms, your nervous system fails your body. We did not get much help from the local medical experts to determine if he had ALS, so we arranged to travel to the Mayo Clinic to find out why Bob kept falling down.

The Mayo Clinic is renowned in medical spheres for its depth of knowledge and expertise in all matters of health diagnostics and care. First we flew to Minneapolis for a stopover and a visit to the fictional Mary Richards' hometown. Our last supper before Bob was to be examined from top to bottom over four days was at Manny's, the best steakhouse in town. Then we drove to the small city of Rochester, Minnesota, most of which is built around the vast downtown campus of the Mayo Clinic.

ALS is determined by a process of elimination of other diseases that have similar symptoms. In Rochester we had a customized itinerary of tests ranging from MRIs, CT scans, blood work and neuropathy probes to interviews and appointments with occupational therapists (how to put on

2 McBeth met a tragic end one weekend at Estergreen. She wandered out to the back field and was attacked by one of the eagles that nested in a tree overlooking the nearby lake. We found her clawed body and buried her in a plain wooden box amongst the heather in the front garden.

your socks) and some education about what ALS was. On our fourth and last day, our quarterbacking doctor gave us the grave news that yes, Bob likely had ALS. There was no cure. Eventually his body would stop functioning; the leg problems would ultimately reach up to his neck and he would stop talking and breathing. And then die of suffocation.

With this depressing news (and US$25,000 later), we drove to Chicago in a snowstorm (the flights were cancelled) and spent a few days enjoying some of the diversions of our favourite American city. Bob braved the trip to the vast Merchandise Mart for the last time to see what was new and what he could use for the custom furnishings he had in mind for clients back in Vancouver. We took in a performance at the Lyric Opera and went to Gibson's for stiff martinis to share a "Chicago Cut" rib-eye (medium rare). Then we went on to Toronto and saw a Canadian Opera production of *The Turn of the Screw*.

When we returned to Vancouver, Bob announced to his staff that he was closing the office due to his diminishing health. Letters of termination were given to each of the employees. He had planned a massive inventory sale for the following month, and by mid-December, Ledingham Design Consultants would be no more. But four four days after he gave notice to his staff, he had a massive stroke and died.

I had lost my partner of over three decades, and I now inherited his business and his twelve employees, three of them unhappy that their jobs were being terminated due to the death of their beloved boss.

(•◆•)

If selling Estergreen was a marathon undertaking, then the winding down of LDC was more like an ironman triathlon, in three parts. The first leg was dealing with the staff and closing the business, the second leg was selling the building and its contents, and the last leg, like a road race with no finish line in sight, was dealing with The Viking.

On my first day on the job as president of LDC, Bob's bookkeeper and office manager presented me with business files. They outlined bank records, accounting details, client lists, staff billings, debts and the status of orders for projects. Most of Bob's work was custom orders for items that could require four or five separate components, mostly imported and quite expensive. A dining chair for a client might involve separate purchase orders for the frame, customized finishing, special fabric, upholstering, plus all the paperwork for shipping, duty and taxes, storage and delivery. There were mountains of paperwork to be coordinated by the staff designer and support staff.

I first had to understand what work was in progress, and for that I arranged interviews with each member of his staff: the office manager, the bookkeeper, four interior designers, an architect, two drafting technicians and one support staff. The receptionist was on maternity leave. During those meetings I reviewed the projects and clients they were working with, their billable hours and their schedules for time off or vacations.

Almost all the staff members were very cooperative, and I did my best to keep things running at the business as I took stock of its viability. I asked that no new orders for goods and furnishings be placed without my consent and requested staff to keep track of their time. The inventory sale Bob had already planned for June would still go ahead, so some staff were tasked with cataloguing, labelling and pricing thousands of items for the sale.

I had considered carrying on the business under the banner of Ledingham Design Consultants, but it became clear after a review of the state of affairs that this plan was not workable. It was Robert Ledingham, and not his staff (or me), whom people wanted to hire. In fact, I learned from the staff interviews that there actually was very little work going on: two of the staff had, on average, two billable hours per month during the previous quarter.

By mid-May I had decided to close the office at the end of July, five months earlier than Bob's original plan. New letters of termination were sent out, and most of the staff agreed to them. Then I took a much-needed break to a wellness retreat to grieve.

When I returned, I learned that someone had convened a staff meeting in my absence to launch a class-action lawsuit for wrongful dismissal. Thankfully, nothing came of that, but the lawyer the disgruntled employee had contacted went on to represent two other staff members with lawsuits. In the end, both were withdrawn or settled.

The inventory sale was successful in clearing out thousands of items that had accumulated in Bob's storerooms over the decades. Stacked on shelves were lamps, accessories, art, cushions and hardware, all stock to be sold to clients. There were Venetian mirrors and Murano glass vases that Bob and I had bought on trips to Venice; beautiful objects made of *shagreen*, *majolica*, silver leaf; and many pieces of Chinese blue-and white porcelain and Japanese *imari*. There were chairs, sofas, tables and custom items that for one reason or another had been returned. There were racks of bolts of end-of-roll fabrics, most costing hundreds of dollars a yard, that were tagged with fire-sale prices. There were bookcases lined with design, art and antique books. Everything had to be listed, priced and tagged.

Besides the items for sale, there was an entire room of fabric and leather samples and another of stone, tiles, wood and carpets. All the suppliers of those products had to be contacted to come and retrieve their samples. Then there were hundreds of design magazines. Decades of back issues of *Architectural Digest, Architectural Record, Arts of Asia, Connoisseur, HALI, Progressive Architecture* and *World of Interiors* were donated to a community college where Bob had taught and hauled off by a student who was a great admirer of him.

All the computers and printers had to be removed. Harder to find homes for were a dozen drafting boards, as by 2013 most work was being done on computers. Habitat for Humanity took them all away, along with dozens of filing cabinets, metal storage shelving, old cans of paint and everything left over from the inventory sales. Rolls and rolls of drawings spanning four decades of Bob's work had to be catalogued. There had been 575 projects over the span of his career. Seventy-four banker boxes of client files were donated to the City of Vancouver Archives. The archivists spent a month on site sorting and cataloguing all that material.

I knew that I needed to sell the building, and I received some good advice on how to market it. The property had become very attractive and had increased in value from when it was first purchased, located as it was in a mixed industrial zone in an emerging neighbourhood of East Vancouver. There were two separate lots, one with the building and the other a surface parking lot, and five months after closing the business I had vacated the building, left it in tidy shape and handed over the keys.

The last leg of the triathlon was a fraud scheme I discovered in one of the files I was given after Bob died. The file was labelled "The Spanish

Endowment Fund" and it contained details of how The Viking had been pestering Bob for money for many years, something I knew nothing about. An RCMP investigation is ongoing a decade later.

(• ◆ •)

After the building sold, I moved my office back to the Barber House and continued to work on conservation projects from there. I wasn't sure what would become of the site at 125 East 4th Avenue, but its development potential was on the cusp of fruition. In the meantime, a prominent landscape architect has taken over the premises of Ledingham Design Consultants, and I recently learned that the partner of the young interior design student who hauled away all those magazines from our office is a landscape architect who works every day in the building that had been Bob's.

I arranged two memorials for Bob. In June, about fifty people – friends, clients and relatives – gathered at Estergreen for an afternoon of remembrances. Al, Bob's older brother, and his niece Donna came from Saskatoon and spoke to the guests. My brother Paul was there, as was Neil Ironside, who travelled from Toronto. It was a beautiful day in the garden with the roses in full bloom.

In the fall there was a larger gathering of almost four hundred people at the Equinox Gallery in Vancouver. All my brothers and their spouses were there, and other guests had come from Toronto, Stratford, Saskatoon and Calgary. I had asked friends and colleagues to speak of Bob's mentorship and devotion to cultural charities. Bob's nephew Greg read a stirring poem he had written for the occasion. My cousin Franki played the cello. The bronze cremation urn I commissioned, from a design by the Seattle architect Tom Kundig, was on display, along with Bob's Lobb oxfords and other mementos of his career.

Bob's talent and influence left a wide imprint in many spheres, and his legacy will remain for years to come in an interior design scholarship program, in a design award in his name at *Western Living* magazine and in the Robert M. Ledingham School of Music, Theatre and Film at Arts Umbrella in Vancouver, which I have endowed.

(•)

WESSEX

"THAT'S MAPPERTON!", I said to myself. Or so I thought, safely muffled in my Air Canada headphones. When the flight attendant peeked into my pod, I realized my renewed enthusiasm for the film had been more vocal than I intended. I had just about given up watching the dreary story of Bathsheba Everdene's life of subservient poverty in rural nineteenth-century Wessex, digging the stony fields for potatoes or turnips in the southwest of Thomas Hardy's England, when she got the letter that changed her life. Bathsheba, played by Carey Mulligan, had inherited the manor house Weatherby, represented by Mapperton House in the 2015 version of *Far From the Madding Crowd*. I continued watching until the plane landed in Toronto.

Mapperton is well known to many from its "open days", when the public could visit the famed Italianate gardens next to this storied fifteenth-century Jacobean manor house. My visits were more private, from times when Bob Ledingham and I were guests there, at the country home of our Vancouver friends John and Jean Hodgins. Well, not actually at the manor house, but at the Rectory, which the Hodginses had leased on the grounds of Mapperton, a short distance from Beaminster in southwest Dorset.

For the better part of the twenty-five years that John and Jean had lived in England, Bob and I had the pleasure of visiting them most summers at their country homes in Dorset. Thomas Hardy wrote extensively about his semi-fictional Wessex, and the places where the Hodginses lived were closely related to some of the places Hardy used as settings for *Tess of the d'Urbervilles*, *Under the Greenwood Tree* and *The Mayor of Casterbridge*.

The Rectory at Mapperton was a handsome building of honey-coloured Ham stone, covered in wisteria. The Italianate gardens at the manor, designed in 1927, have been featured in *Country Life* and are among the finest in England according to the garden guru Christopher Lloyd. We were privileged to be able to enjoy them privately.

The Wessex, or rather Dorset, stories started with weekend visits to Mapperton. Most years, sometime in March, Jean would phone from London to say that she and John had scored tickets to Glyndebourne, the summer opera festival in Sussex, and could Bob and I come in June? We never said no.

(• ◆ •)

Our trips to Wessex began with a Thursday night departure from Vancouver on a British Airways flight to London, landing around midday on Friday, when we would be met at Heathrow by George, Jean and John's local driver, who would take us on the three-hour journey to Dorset. George was a stalwart of the Hodginses' life there, reliable to a fault, and usually two or three hours early to meet us at Heathrow. He was also very talkative. After an hour or so of his banter in an almost indecipherable Dorset accent, we would feign jet lag and nod off in the back seat, perking up as our journey along the A3 took us by Stonehenge and the Salisbury Plain. Then it was eyes closed again until we arrived at the Hodginses' home at the Mapperton Rectory.

Jean was a very good cook, and I can recall every morsel of food she ever prepared. I recall one Friday arrival dinner of lamb stew with *haricot vertes* and lots of excellent wine, followed by my lone annual cigar as I joined John for a postprandial tour of Mapperton's sunken Italian garden.

Saturdays started with breakfast, where John would master the AGA with sausages, scrambled eggs and toast, accompanied by Jean's marmalade. Then we were busy with errands in the countryside or excursions to see gardens such as Hadspen, East Lambrook or Hestercombe. We often had a gastropub lunch or a visit with their friends John and Ginny Makepeace at Parnham, their school of modern furniture design in Beaminster.

For dinner on Saturday night, John and Jean would invite some of their circle of local friends who gardened, were artists, rode and hunted and occasionally shot birds. One delightful elderly couple told us about their holiday, not a package trip to the Costa del Sol but an arduous tour of stave churches in rural Romania. On the Weber kettle grill, brought from Vancouver, John would produce a perfectly grilled local butterflied lamb, marinated in Jean's recipe of garlic, lemon juice, rosemary and olive oil. Our assignment was to bring the Ziploc bags from Vancouver for the marinating, as until recently they were not to be found in England. Every crunchy bit of grilled lamb would be eaten up that same night.

As the location was not far from West Bay and Bridport on Dorset's south coast, very good seafood was available. One Saturday for lunch, Jean made a green mayonnaise, dense with parsley and basil, to have with fresh cold Dorset lobster. West Bay was noted for the Riverside Restaurant (now closed), where we spent most of a leisurely Sunday afternoon over a delicious fish lunch with a table full of their local friends. Bill Bryson, in his travels around England, stumbled upon the same place, and Olivia Colman has been there recently, as *Broadchurch* was filmed in West Bay.

Later, when the Hodginses took a lease on an eighteenth-century farmhouse at Lower Holt Farm on the Ilchester Estate next to Melbury House near Evershot (another Hardy film locale), I had the pleasure of helping reconfigure a tangle of small rooms to make a comfortable home for them within the walls of a handsome stone and thatched-roofed building. The place was an old farmhouse, listed as Grade II by English Heritage, that had been built and extended over many years. It was laid out in a T-shape, two storeys high, with the eighteenth-century part at the top of the T, running parallel to the steep slope of the property. The stem of the T was also of stone, with a slate roof, and stepped down the slope to the rutted lane, lined with hedgerows, which was their road access. The part of the house closest to the road contained service rooms, including a pantry, larder, garage and several potting rooms that opened to a walled garden. Enclosing their garden were stone barns and outbuildings of the former farmstead, which would eventually be renovated for leasehold holiday homes.

When I discovered that slabs of old stones extended under the warren of wooden partitions, I knew that I had the interior redesign figured out.

I had the approval of the estate architect to rearrange the interior spaces as long as there were no exterior changes. My plan was to remove all of the small rooms in the centre section of the building and make a central "hall", with windows on two sides and the old stone floor slabs exposed as they had been originally. This would be the Hodginses' entry hall and dining room. The kitchen, with its vintage AGA, was kept where it was and updated with new cabinetry and lighting. The two rooms in the oldest wing became sitting rooms, one for morning and one for evening, the latter being spacious enough for Jean's grand piano. Each room had a fireplace, the morning room's elegant and rather Georgian while the evening room's was much older and almost medieval in scale (I am over six feet tall and could just fit under the mantle). John was a master at laying and tending a roaring blaze after a leisurely dinner in the dining hall.

The interior improvements were carried out to the letter, except for one detail which I discovered when I went down to Dorset to view the progress of the works. Everything was in order. Opening up the central part of the building for the dining hall looked even better than I had imagined, and Jean and John were thrilled. The new cabinetry in the kitchen was lovely, and the new lighting made a huge difference to the space. In the morning sitting room, the base coat of raw plaster was about to be painted over. It looked just like polished *stucco lustro*, a subtle pale pink colour which was

the tint of the local clay. Sadly, my appeals to leave it as was, beautiful and unpainted, went unheeded.

On a subsequent visit with Bob, as we spent the morning in that room reading the Sunday papers, I held my tongue about how much more lovely it would have been with the rosy glow of natural polished plaster. That was the occasion when Jean prepared a lovely lunch of roast partridge on a garlic-buttered crouton from an Elizabeth David recipe. After lunch, with John out in the garden and Jean upstairs napping, Bob and I decided to take charge of rearranging the furniture of the two sitting rooms. Perhaps it's the curse of the designer's eyes, but we agreed that the current arrangement was all wrong. When Jean came down and saw the transformation she was gobsmacked, in a good way. The furnishings stayed where we had moved them – I think because they liked the improved arrangement, or perhaps because moving it all back would have been too much work.

One of our trips to England coincided with a trip with Tom and Dave, our friends from Los Angeles ("Just off Melrose"), and we had all been invited to spend the weekend at Lower Holt Farm. The four of us drove down to Dorset the day before the Hodginses came down from London by train, so we took charge of the meal to welcome our hosts. That meant shopping for local lamb at the butcher shop in Sherborne, a short drive away, which we planned to grill on John's Weber, annointed with rosemary brushes plucked from his herb garden, something Tom knew as a Martha Stewart idea. We scoured the countryside for flowers for the table and found wild poppies at the abandoned Upper Holt Farm. For dessert, I picked tart cherries from a tree overhanging the lane from the churchyard in Melbury Osmond, the hamlet nearby. Little did we know what a fuss the

locals would make as apparently it was just not done to pick wild poppies
or overhanging fruit.

(•♦•)

Glyndebourne is known for its productions of baroque to modern and
sometimes controversial opera, performed in a glorious country house
setting. The experience involves formal dress, taking a train from London
down to Lewes in Sussex, quaffing champagne and a posh "picnic" in the
garden during the long interval. In a beautiful new building designed by
Hopkins Architects we saw productions of *Rodelinda*, *Capriccio* (with Kiri
Te Kanawa) and a stark version of *Don Giovanni* featuring a stage covered
with a slagheap of asphalt and the carcass of a dead horse that elicited boos
from the equine-loving audience.

We were reminded that we had made a journey halfway around the
world specifically to attend a Glyndebourne production one year when
Bob and I arrived at the theatre very late for the performance. We could see
Jean, in a lovely gown and wrapped in a pashmina, fuming on the upper
terrace while John, smartly dressed in black tie and smoking a Davidoff
cigar, paced below with the champagne cooler and tickets in hand. Earlier
that day in London, around noon on a Wednesday, Bob and I had dressed

in the dinner jackets we brought for the occasion, then took a cab from our friends' Bayswater flat to Waterloo Station for the short train ride to Lewes. When we arrived at Waterloo, we were puzzled not to find the Hodginses (who had the opera tickets) or anyone else in tuxedos making their way to Lewes. It didn't take long to realize that we were at the wrong station.

A helpful British Rail officer directed us to hail a cab for Victoria Station. With scant time to spare we arrived at Victoria and were informed by another sharp British Rail agent to hop on "that express train to Brighton *right now*". We ran to the rear platform – without tickets – just as it left the station, and by some miracle we got to Brighton just as the connecting local train was about to head north one stop to Lewes. Perhaps it was a mercy that I had forgotten my watch so had no idea what time it was, and as John had the tickets we had no idea of the curtain time. To add to the worry, in the time before mobile phones, the Hodginses had no idea of our predicament. Arriving at Lewes and forging ahead rather blindly, we got a taxi and headed out to the Glyndebourne estate, only to be stuck in road works. We finally arrived, to be greeted with glares of disapproval, but thankfully the whole performance was delayed because of the same road works.

I cannot recall the opera, but I do recall the beautiful new theatre with its intimate scale – 1,200 seats in a tiered horseshoe shape – wrapped in warm wood panelling. All was well by the time we arrived at the long interval, when we enjoyed a picnic on the lawn set up by a butler serving us champagne, poached lobster and Eton mess, that traditional English dessert of meringue, whipped cream and fresh strawberries.

(◆◆◆)

Our Dorset trips were also memorable for visits to friends of John and Jean's who lived in beautiful historic houses with names like Melplash Court, Little Benville House, Parnham House, Wooth and Wraxall Manors and Wyndom. Often we were invited for drinks or dinner, and on a few occasions for an overnight or weekend stay. Most of the houses are mentioned in *The Buildings of England: Dorset.*

On one occasion we were invited to tour Melbury House, the country manor that is the seat of the vast Ilchester Estate, which includes Lower Holt Farm. It had a long history in Wessex, being mentioned in the Domesday Book in 1086 and the family lineage is notable for bucking the male-dominated primogeniture pattern. The estate includes the villages of Evershot, Melbury Osmond and a wide swath of the south coast of Dorset. There is even a swannery, as the Honourable Charlotte Townshend, doyenne of Melbury, is the only person in Britain who is entitled to own swans aside from the Queen.

At Melbury we first toured the grounds, with its deer park, ice pond and icehouse, extensive gardens, arboretum and lake that was said to have been

laid out by Humphry Repton, the noted eighteenth-century landscape designer, and a private chapel called Melbury Sampford. The 15,000 acres of Ilchester are linked to the estate's land holdings in London's Holland Park, where Ilchester Place is one of the country's poshest addresses.

After the tour of the grounds of Melbury, we were offered a glass of wine on the terrace overlooking the lake. There was a bowl of speckled pheasant eggs, hard-boiled, to be peeled and dipped in a dish of curry powder. Inside the house were Grinling Gibbons carved panellings, a room just for a vast collection of majolica, a magnificent dining room where their lurchers, the dogs often kept in country houses, could roam and defecate behind the curtains (the English quaintly refer to the heavily bumpf-lined and chain-weighted drapes as "curtains"), and a stair hall lined with family pictures (which is what the English call paintings), several of them by Hogarth.

My last memory of that visit is of leafing through the guest book which sat on a table in the entrance hall. There, around about 1902, was the signature of Thomas Hardy.

(• ◆ •)

Over the years, the Hodginses' very comfortable homes in the hills of Wessex were like second homes for Bob and me, and the highlight of many visits to Britain. One year on Boxing Day, Bob and I flew to Heathrow and then on to Dorset to spend a week with them at Lower Holt Farm to celebrate Jean's birthday. In my luggage were two litres of frozen lobster stock that I had made from the crustaceans Bob's niece Donna sent every year as a Christmas gift when she was studying medicine at Dalhousie University in Halifax. I was going to make the soup for the birthday dinner John had arranged for Jean. It was a party of sixteen seated at a long table in the dining hall I had designed for them. The squash soup I made with the lobster stock was garnished with Dorset lobster claws. The caterer had made the main course of beef tenderloin, but Jean made the dessert herself. It was her favourite, a shortbread cookie crust, spread over a sheet pan and scored into portions. Once cooked it was smeared with melted chocolate. Then a fan of sliced poached pears was arranged on top of each portion. With the excellent wines John had decanted and the lively conversation, the meal was deemed a triumph.

After the pomp of the birthday dinner we brought in the New Year in the quietest possible way. Then the four of us flew to Venice for a splendid four days, enjoying alternating sun and fog, to celebrate Epiphany. The times spent with John and Jean in Dorset, London, Madrid and Venice are cherished.

(•♦•)

When the Hodginses moved back to Vancouver, I was honoured to be asked to design their summer home on one of the southern Gulf Islands. They gave me *carte blanche* on the design, as long as I got the kitchen right for Jean. She always commented when she was there how much they loved their modern west coast retreat.

(•♦•)

Jean Elizabeth Hodgins (née Mercer) was a musician, a musicologist and Benjamin Britten scholar. She relished her time in England both musically and artistically and studied at the Britten Pears Library in Aldeburgh and Kings College, London then coordinated the Modern Art Studies program at Christies Auction House in London. She invited Bob and me to music programs in London that ranged from opera to chamber music. When she returned to Vancouver, she became the president of the Vancouver Recital Society and invited me to join her for a dinner at Bishop's - perhaps the best restaurant in Vancouver – after Murray Perahia (her favourite pianist) had performed. She relished the house (and kitchen) I designed for her at the island house.

Jean died in February 2022 after a 35-year battle with cancer. I will miss very much and remember not just her delicious meals but her critical eye and enthusiasm for music and the arts.

(﹡)

TWELFTH AND CAMBIE

"WE'RE NOT HAPPY 'til you're not happy". That was one of the inside jokes that a very talented, conscientious (and droll) co-worker let me in on when I shifted my career to a stint as a city hall bureaucrat.

In the spring of 1991, Jacquie Forbes-Roberts,[1] Vancouver's heritage planner, called to ask if I would agree to take her position at city hall for six months as she was being promoted to a senior management position. I thought it would be an interesting prospect, rather like a working sabbatical, so I agreed, put my architectural practice on hold and went to work as a planner. I ended up as senior heritage planner, heading the team of five in the heritage group of the planning department, and staying there for five and a half years.

---

1 It was Jacquie who had called about rescuing the Barber House the very day we planned to see it.

Vancouver's city hall is a striking landmark of Art Moderne design, dating to 1936 and exactly contemporary in style and date with the Barber House. Perched on a slope overlooking the city at the corner of Twelfth Avenue and Cambie Street, its prominence displayed the progress of the city when it was completed to mark the fiftieth anniversary of the founding of Vancouver. Although my office in the planning department was in an annex built in the 1970s, I was proud to work for a city that had such a splendid historic city hall.

As much as architects gripe about dealing with bureaucracies, I would recommend that any of them try a stint on the other side of the counter at city hall. Once I was "inside", I found it intriguing to navigate the civic administration and to see just how decisions are made. Aside from the purely heritage portfolio, as a senior planner I was at the table for the review of most of the major projects that were working their way through the city's planning process. I was even asked to be part of the review of the three submissions in competition for Vancouver's new public library. The winning candidate was Moshe Safdie's modern take on Rome's coliseum which was most popular with the public and the mayor despite the staff preference for another scheme.

Old buildings rarely conform to regulations imposed after they were built. Modern planning and zoning rules never set a level playing field, so my primary responsibility, and that of my group of planners and architects in the heritage program, was to advocate and to help the owners of these buildings through the system of zoning and code building conflicts. I also felt that it was important to change some of those rules.

During my time at city hall, I oversaw a survey of post-World War II buildings which became the Recent Landmarks inventory. A modernist building's presence on that list would provide access to incentives such as those enjoyed by the older buildings on the heritage register. I was able to persuade many of the owners of those one hundred buildings to allow them to be added to the official Vancouver Heritage Register, including Dr. and Mrs. Copp's Ron Thom-designed house (1951), Arthur Erickson's MacMillan Bloedel building (1968) and the quietly elegant Unitarian Church (1964) by Wolfgang Gerson.

I was tasked with addressing new provincial heritage legislation, as it would involve amending the Vancouver Charter. That legislation opened up a whole new range of incentives and also allowed for the protection of landscapes and interiors. Anticipating the inclusion of interiors in the legislation, I sourced city and provincial funding for a survey of important interiors in the city's public and private buildings. The survey, prepared by Don Luxton, was called "Take a Look Inside" and it is referenced to this day when conservation work is proposed for buildings. In my post-city hall work, I have restored or conserved important heritage-protected interiors at the Hotel Georgia and the Shannon Estate (see "125 East 4th Avenue").

One heritage incentive that was already on the books, the Transfer of Heritage Density Policy, had seldom been used since it was instituted in the mid-1980s. Christ Church Cathedral, an historic but modest stone structure on a prominent downtown site, was the oldest church in the city. It was threatened with demolition to make way for an office tower, with a new church incorporated in the podium. Instead, the unused density (called "airspace" in cities like New York and Seattle) was sold to the property next door to add to its height and size. But rare were the circumstances of a heritage building with an adjacent site that could take over the airspace in one rezoning process. My task, aided by a supporting team of planners and real estate professionals in-house, was to broaden the parameters of the area within which density could be transferred (i.e., sold) to another downtown site some distance away.

The updated Transfer of Density Policy was approved by the city council and in the late 1990s resulted in the conservation of some of the city's prominent modernist buildings, including the BC Electric Building (now the Elektra condos), the former Vancouver Public Library and Stanley Theatre.[2]

There were champions of heritage conservation within the planning staff, in addition to Jacquie's continued watch from a management position. Larry Beasley was very supportive of heritage conservation, and my experience working on guidelines for Chinatown led to his inviting me to join the team in Xi'an. The senior development planner was Ralph Segal, with whom I shared an interest in how new and old could co-exist. Rick Scobie, in charge of development approvals and subdivisions, used his red pen liberally over the reports to city council that I drafted. Most needed special zoning concessions, and Rick was fair in adjudicating matters that needed the interpretation of regulations.

Working with me in the heritage group were Jeannette Hlavach, an experienced planner, and Gerry McGeough,[3] an architect, all of us ably assisted

2 The Stanley Theatre was preserved by having its unused density sold and transferred to a downtown site.

3 Gerry went on to be the campus architect at the University of British Columbia.

by planning assistant Marco D'Agostino.[4] Between us we kept the agendas for the Vancouver Heritage Commission, Gastown and Chinatown heritage area advisory committees, and the Shaughnessy design panel filled with heritage projects that were in the system for review. We usually had to convince our colleagues in the engineering, building or real estate departments why heritage buildings needed special consideration. They might represent the city's history or be of architectural interest, but they also contributed to the emerging narrative of sustainability in the mid-1990s.

As part of my job, I gave many talks to community groups, explaining what heritage was all about and why Vancouver's buildings were valued. I worked closely with the City Program at Simon Fraser University's downtown campus to arrange workshops on subjects ranging from the seismic retrofit of heritage buildings (shortly after the Loma Prieta earthquake), conserving architectural terra cotta (led by my mentor Martin Weaver) and colour in the city (led by Bente Lange). This collaboration with SFU paved the way for the "True Colours" granting program at the Vancouver Heritage Foundation.

But my first and possibly most important file at city hall, arriving shortly after I started to work there in mid-1991, was the creation of what became

---

4 Marco worked his way up to the Planner III position I once held.

the Vancouver Heritage Foundation. A prominent mansion in Shaughnessy Heights, Glen Brae, had been donated to the city for public and heritage purposes. The city manager realized that such a donation should properly be held by a foundation or trust, so working with the city's consulting lawyer, I worked on the mandate and bylaws for the creation of such a foundation. It was launched in 1992 with a board composed of the mayor and city council, which was later amended to be a board of volunteer community members appointed by the city council under an executive director. When it was refreshed in that form in 1998, after my departure from city hall in 1996, I was appointed to the inaugural slate of board members.

(•♦•)

Before I close this chapter, I will relate one delightful memory of my time at Vancouver city hall. As a registered architect working as a planner, I was required to belong to the union. During a rotating strike at city hall, the support staff were off the job, and a manager was answering the phones. As he handed me a pile of pink phone message slips, he said that I got more phone calls than any other staff member. On another occasion, one of those calls caught me by surprise. I picked up the receiver and the caller identified himself as Philip Owen (the mayor – the one who came to the Barber House party not the previous one, who picked the library design).

The mayor of Vancouver was asking me for advice on some heritage matter that was before city council. He also took the time to come to my farewell luncheon at my favourite Szechuan restaurant near city hall.

The stories about my life and work at city hall could fill another book, and perhaps I will leave that chapter of my life to this outline for now. Once my stint as a bureaucrat was over, I returned to my architectural practice at 125 East 4th Avenue.

(•♦•)

There is more to say about the Vancouver Heritage Foundation.

After I left Twelfth and Cambie I continued to be involved with the VHF, first when I was appointed by city council to be on the inaugural board of directors when my architect colleague Joost Bakker was chair. The sale of the modernist Vancouver Public Library and its development rights had netted a substantial fund (the real estate broker donated half the commission) earmarked for an endowment for the VHF. Yet the board struggled to create an identity for the VHF beyond a general notion of helping with the conservation of Vancouver's heritage buildings. I proposed a granting program for the owners of heritage houses to paint them in their original colours, based on Bente Lange's *Colours of Rome* methodology. The result was the "True Colours" program sponsored by Benjamin Moore where research was done on each house to determine the original colour scheme. Paint scraping and sample analysis was done, coordinated by Don Luxton, then Benjamin Moore developed specific new paint colours, named for the locales of the buildings and the architectural styles prevalent in Vancouver from the late 19th century to the mid 1920s ranging from Victorian to Queen Anne, Edwardian, Craftsman and Tudor Revival. Hence Pendrell Cream, Dunbar Buff, Mount Pleasant Tan, Strathcona Red, Kitsilano Gold and Point Grey. Homeowners would receive free paint and a grant to help with the painting work.

Another initiative in the early years of the VHF was the Heritage and Antiques Fair which was held for three years starting in 1999 at the historic Seaforth Armoury in Vancouver. It was a massive undertaking for a small organization. Over 10,000 people attended the weekend fair each spring which was kicked off with a gala evening event. Dozens of booths were rented to tradespeople, suppliers and antiques dealers and there was a local version of the "Antiques Road Show" booth. I was co-chair with Mamie Angus one year.

Inspired by the Open Days tours of Sydney in 2002, I helped set up the first Open Vancouver Heritage House Tour for the VHF in 2003, something that has carried on each year since. In 2006 Mamie Angus' house was featured with the kitchen I designed for her inspired by Lutyens' Castle Drogo pantry. The VHF also offered tours of some of the remarkable mid-century modern houses in the city and I coaxed the owners of houses by Dan White, the Patkaus, Arthur Erickson and the Oberlanders to open their doors. The Barber House was included too. For several years I served as the chair of the board while the Founding Pillars endowment campaign was launched. Later I co-chaired the major gifts campaign.

As I write this, the VHF is celebrating its thirtieth anniversary and I am proud to have been involved since its inception. As the organization has remained focussed on promoting heritage conservation through education it has been able to punch above its weight by helping tell the story of Vancouver's history and the value that its past has for a growing city.

(♦)

JUST OFF MELROSE

JUST OFF MELROSE on the border of Los Angeles and West Hollywood is a pair of white stucco buildings encrusted with minarets, Moorish arches and wrought iron, and topped with domes – a fantasy of Moroccan design. The buildings are a local landmark and well known to Angelinos, and they belong to my friends Tom and Dave.

Bob Ledingham travelled to Los Angeles quite regularly to source furnishings and fabrics for his interior design business, and I often tagged along. On one such trip we retreated to the desert, where we met Tom at a bar in Palm Springs – he had come over to say we were both overdressed for the down-at-the-heels bar. Tom was very tall, perfectly groomed and very entertaining. He and his husband, Dave, had escaped the winters of Detroit for the year-round warmth of L.A., and we developed a wonderful, if long-distance, friendship.

Tom Thomas was in the women's fashion business based in L.A., and Dave Duyck sold women's shoes at Neiman Marcus in Beverley Hills. They lived a life of high style and extravagance that was the opposite of ours in staid Vancouver. They always had the right posh car – one year it was a vintage white Jaguar with red leather seats – so that when they pulled up to the latest restaurant, it would impress the parking valets.

After that introduction, our trips to L.A. always included visits with Tom and Dave. We were invited and honoured guests at many of their lavish Easter feasts where Tom, of Greek descent and an excellent cook, prepared all the food for their over-the-top parties. Dave's mother would have hand-made the table linens themed to the long-table alfresco dinner each year and sent them from Detroit.

(•♦•)

I have never lived in Los Angeles, nor would I ever choose to do so. Nice as it is to visit, a close up few days is enough for me. The pressure to be perfectly groomed all the time, to look youthful and dress stylishly, to dine in the latest restaurant and have the right car would be exhausting. I have trouble keeping track of sunglasses and hate wearing them anyway. However, our occasional visits with Tom and Dave had a bit of Hollywood magic. And intrigue.

When we met, Tom and Dave owned one of the two Moroccan houses at the corner of Waring and Sweetzer Avenues. They lived in the upper-floor flat they had renovated stylishly and surrounded with beautiful Mediterranean gardens. Sadly, the mirror-image twin house next door had seen better days. W.C. Fields was rumoured to have had the pair built as a revenue property. What is certain is that they date to 1926 and are the work of Carl Kay, an architect originally from Armenia, who worked in a style called Islamic Revival. They fit perfectly in a neighbourhood filled with around-the-world stylistic fantasy apartment buildings – Spanish mission, Italianate villa, French chateau, Cotswold cottage, you name it. As if that were not architectural pedigree enough, Rudolf Schindler's modernist house and garden from 1922 – now an historic site curated by UCLA and the Viennese MAC foundation – is just a block away.

Tom and Dave had been watching the vacant building next door to theirs for some time. One weekend while we were visiting, they invited us to take a look into the vacant house; the kitchen door was unlocked. The scale and stench of the contents was breathtaking. The interior was stacked literally to the ceiling with magazines, newspapers, books, clothes, shoes, furniture, dishes and everything else only a hoarder could cherish. Food had been rotting in the refrigerator for years. We squirmed when we unearthed a Rubbermaid washtub filled with dildos, then retreated to Tom and Dave's house to wash our hands.

The owner had been in the movie business, had disappeared and was rumoured to have suffered some kind of drug-related death, so when the house was put up for auction in 1994 by the city for back taxes, Tom and Dave were prompt in bidding. They ended up as the new owners, where-upon they embarked on the herculean task of clearing out the contents. First they had to carve narrow paths from room to room amongst the towering stash of junk. It took four weekend yard sales to get rid of all the salvageable stuff, and on the last weekend, Bob and I joined them and helped with the final sale. What remained on that last Saturday – including hundreds of mismatched women's shoes – was left on the boulevard overnight. By Sunday morning it was all gone, having been taken by scavengers.

Yet there were treasures amongst the trash, as the long-gone owner had amassed an impressive collection of Moroccan furniture, books, ceramics, textiles and beautiful architectural elements. There were large wooden frames of Moorish archways, screens and panelling that had probably come from Hollywood movie sets. Dave meticulously catalogued and measured them all.

Given the style and panache of their lifestyle, I was thrilled when they asked me to design the renovation for their newly acquired building and was even happier when they carried it out to the letter. My task as their architect was to redesign the interior and incorporate all the wooden artefacts. Most of the house would become a two-storey townhouse for them, with space for a pair of small rental studios in the rear. I had a pretty good idea of how to incorporate all the Moroccan doors, frames, arches and lattice panels.

The redesign started with sketches I did on one weekend visit as I spent a lazy afternoon poolside at the Beverly Hills Hotel, getting inspired by the glamour of southern California. One of the bold suggestions I offered, not thinking it would actually be realized, was to convert the dilapidated garage into a dining room. I said it would be lovely lined with fabric, like a Bedouin tent. They took me seriously and covered every wall and the vaulted ceiling with hundreds of yards of paisley-patterned chintz.

With the garage converted to the dining room, the driveway area became a courtyard with a fountain filled with turtles. The entrance to the house was changed by creating a new foyer from what was originally a tiny dining room. The original entry turret became a circular powder room with an alabaster floor, lit from below. Tom and Dave are the only clients who have taken my suggestion of a lit-from-below alabaster floor seriously. The salvaged Moorish wooden arches and panelled doors were positioned to frame the living room. Upstairs, more wooden screens divided the master bedroom from the bathroom. The roof of the garage became a garden. And the top of the entry turret was a lookout beneath the stuccoed minaret.

In a way, Tom and Dave were also hoarders, but with the most exquisite taste. Why their home has not been featured in *World of Interiors* is a mystery.

For years they had been accumulating furnishings, ceramics, decorative objects, pierced metal lanterns and *objets d'art* that showed Arabic influences. When it came to furnishing their new home, they found places for pieces of marquetry, inlaid mother-of-pearl, *cloisonné* enamel and their vast collection of *majolica*, beautifully displayed in tablescapes augmented by Tom's orchid collection. Many things they had scored from Neiman Marcus window displays or at auctions of Hollywood collectors, such as that of Tony Duquette, the artist and set designer. The parties they hosted were memorable.

When asked where they lived, Tom and Dave would say, "We live in those Moroccan houses, just off Melrose". Most people knew exactly where that was.

(•♦•)

We travelled together as well, first to London, Dorset, Belgium and the Netherlands, and then another trip to Greece and Turkey. Finally we managed to spend two weeks together exploring Morocco. The four of us toured the country with a guide and driver, seeing the maze of streets in Fez and the Roman ruins at Volubilis, driving through the Atlas Mountains to see my favourite tree, the blue Atlas cedar (*cedra Atlantica*), up close, staying in an old fort in the desert and luxuriating in the villas at La Gazelle d'Or. We ate in smart restaurants, at roadside cafes, in dusty tagine shops and out in the desert in a bespoke campsite set up just for us where we rode camels at dawn the next morning. Then at the posh La Mamounia hotel in Marrakesh we overindulged in the seafood buffet, and most of us got food poisoning. One of the joys of travel is having a good story of survival in the lap of luxury.

(♦)

XI'AN

E ACH NIGHT WHEN I returned to the hotel, Peter was outside on the front steps with his shoeshine kit. I really did need frequent shoe shining, having trudged the filthy lanes and courtyards of the historic Muslim quarter, which left a residue of late-winter grime on my shoes, but mostly I enjoyed our brief evening chats. My Mandarin was limited to a few tentative greetings, so we conversed in English, which he spoke very well, though when he learned I was from Canada, he often switched to French. He also had a smattering of German, and he was used to engaging with foreign tourists, most of whom came to Xi'an to see the terra cotta warriors.

Peter wanted to practise his English, and I was happy to hear what it was like to live in late-twentieth-century China. He worked on the streets of Xi'an, selling prints and trinkets and shining shoes for foreigners, a sign of China's rapid emergence from the protection of a communist regime to a new reality that embraced capitalism. He was still a teenager and had to make a living for himself and his family, something that had not been required in the past.

I must admit that until I travelled to China, I had scant knowledge of the country and its history. Like most westerners I knew of Xi'an primarily because of the army of terra cotta warriors uncovered nearby in 1974. But had no idea of the historic role Xi'an played as an Imperial City or its importance related to the Silk Road. That there was a sizable Muslim population in China had never occurred to me.

(•♦•)

Heritage conservation and public engagement were also new to Xi'an – and to an emerging China – and that is why I was there in March 1998 as part of a small team of Canadian planners invited to work with the local government on the preservation of Xi'an's historic Muslim district.

By the late twentieth century, the Chinese philosophy for dealing with old buildings was either careful and often heavy-handed "restoration" or completely new "reconstruction" after demolition. My expertise as an architect was on a middle ground called "rehabilitation", where the best of the old is retained and repaired while allowing for modern innovations such as plumbing. Touring the historic but dense and often squalid quarters was eye-opening, as many families and shopkeepers were crammed into courtyard houses that were the once spacious single-family homes. And it was sobering to see that people who had telephones and televisions in their houses – tuned to *Baywatch*, no less – often had no plumbing or heating. The ground of the rear, mostly private, courtyards of the traditional homes was often used for the latrine. In mid-March, the shops lining the narrow lanes of the quarter, open to the air, had braziers burning pellets of coal for heat. The air was thick with a pale gray ash from the fires, worsened by the sand blowing east from the Gobi Desert.

Our hotel was situated opposite the Bell Tower, at the nexus of the street grid that cuts the historic centre of this former Imperial City into

quadrants. Xi'an's immense ramparts are still largely intact and surrounded by a grassed-in moat. The tapered brick walls, fifteen to eighteen metres thick at the base, stretch four kilometres in one direction and three in the other. Dating back to the much earlier history of the Qin dynasty, the twelve-square-kilometre enclosure marked the extent of just the Imperial Palace in the fourteenth century.

A short walk from the Bell Tower was the Drum Tower, the two structures reminders of Xi'an's dominance in the sixteenth century, positioned strategically on the eastern edge of the Gobi Desert and at the start (or end, I suppose, depending on one's perspective) of the legendary Silk Road across Asia. The Drum Tower was at the southern edge of a maze of streets, alleys and courtyard houses built of dark grey brick with elaborate wooden decorations that made up the Muslim district. This historic area was now overcrowded and in a sad state of decline, but it was also safeguarded from demolition due to the cultural sensitivities the Chinese regime had for the Muslim population. This was why I had come to advise on the ways and means to conserve the fabric and history of the network of historic courtyard buildings.

(•♦•)

"Is it Baccarat?" I queried with a grin as we descended the grand staircase to the hotel lobby on our way to work one morning. The shimmering cascade of glass that made up the massive chandelier pretty much expressed the design aspirations of the rapidly developing country. By 1998, vast stretches of buildings within Xi'an's walled city had been bulldozed and replaced with shiny, gaudy and colourful buildings, each screaming for attention. The Bell Tower Hotel was more sober, being the product of an earlier era of development in China when Xi'an was pegged as a special destination by the governing regime.

Our work with the local planners was led by Gao Xiaoji, a woman in her mid-thirties, part of a cohort of 16,000 municipal staff for this city of about 8 million people. Their keen interest in their rich and storied history and their respect for tradition were evident in many ways. But the gap between the reverence for history and the appreciation of the tangible fabric of heritage was enormous.

The official title of our project was "Application of Canadian Techniques in Planning for a New Approach to Historic Preservation in Xi'an, The Peoples Republic of China". What this meant was that we were outlining techniques common in Canada and the Western world, but unknown in Communist China, such as inviting stakeholders to the table. This was unheard of in China, where master planning was entirely top down, and our work was ground-breaking.

Reading my diary of the trip refreshed my memory of those days much more than the few photos I took. I had constant problems with my camera, and I seemed to be searching for a camera repair shop every other day. When the camera was working, the light meter had a hard time registering, as the atmosphere of late-winter Xi'an was thick with pale gray smog. The one day when the city turned serene and stunningly beautiful during a snowfall, I escaped to the courtyards of the Great Mosque to see it covered in a light dusting of pale gray snow. Sadly, my camera once again balked. Yet the memory of exploring this beautiful place on a quiet snowy morning is more detailed than anything a photo-graph could capture.

The fourteenth-century Great Mosque is at the centre of the Muslim district, and in all but a few details it resembles a magnificent Chinese

temple. Where a Buddhist temple would be oriented south, for example, the Mosque faced west towards Mecca. The inscriptions on the buildings and the surrounding dark gray stone stele are in Arabic. A series of beautifully landscaped courtyards was separated by pavilions with glazed turquoise tiled roofs, turned-up horned eaves, red-painted columns and a minaret designed just like a bell tower.

(◆ ◆ ◆)

The project had begun two years earlier in 1996 when Larry Beasley, then the co-director of planning for the City of Vancouver, and Louise Morris of Canada's Open Cities program (an arm of the Federation of Canadian Municipalities International Office) had travelled to Xi'an to scope out a project of heritage conservation and public consultation. The following year a team of planners from Xi'an came to Vancouver for a series of workshops, and I was invited to participate. As senior heritage planner for the City of Vancouver in the early 1990s, I had worked closely with Larry on many heritage initiatives, one of them being design guidelines for Vancouver's historic Chinatown, which was a reference point for the engagement of the two cities. While the architectural heritage of the two places was very different, the overlap of cultural values was useful.

For the third phase of the project, our small team was invited to travel to Xi'an to work with the local planning and engineering departments. Over ten days we led a series of workshops to establish a plan for public consultation, civic engagement and design guidelines for the conservation of the buildings and area.

For long days we sat in a conference room, sometimes in darkness when there were power failures, in what was perhaps the first time in China that the input of citizenry had been sought in a planning process. There were two main threads to our working assignment: first, to show the local

government how to consult and listen to the needs of the community when making planning decisions, and then to teach them how to develop design guidelines to conserve and rehabilitate their stock of historic buildings. Explaining the difference between restoration, rehabilitation and replication was the task of Jennifer Hsu, our expert interpreter, and we quickly learned the value of having someone from Vancouver, fluent in Mandarin, accompanying us, not only to translate our words for the Chinese, but at the same time to interpret their comprehension of the proceedings. Her mastery of the local dialect was so impressive that several people from the Xi'an team thought she was a native. At the end of each day, we would retreat to our hotel to summarize the discussions, translate our findings into Chinese and prepared acetate sheets for the overhead projector we used to recap to the group the next day.

(•♦•)

There were two visits to Beijing, the first immediately upon arrival from Vancouver, when we had a short stay and a whirlwind tour of the Forbidden City and Tiananmen Square. I mostly remember the Peking duck we ate one night. The second visit to the capital took place after our work was finished in Xi'an, when I had a layover en route to Shanghai. After seeing the courtyard houses of Xi'an, I was eager to see the courtyard Hutong houses of Beijing that were once common all over the city. They had a shop facing the street with a narrow passage that led to a courtyard, then a dwelling and another courtyard. Usually topped by a second or sometimes a third storey, this house form provided dense but liveable, well-ventilated and beautiful buildings for centuries. In 1998 when I was there, only one street remained to serve as an example, largely as a tourist attraction.

Then I was off to Shanghai, where I was excited to see its legacy of Art Deco architecture and the Lilong houses that were quickly disappearing. The many European "concessions" had left their architectural mark on this fascinating city, and the Lilongs were different from other historic Chinese dwellings, more a product of the profound influence Western culture had on Shanghai, a sort of hybrid of the traditional courtyard houses of Xi'an and Beijing, with an overlay of London's terrace houses and mews. Led by my guide Chen Yi, an architecture professor in Shanghai, I was allowed to see a neighbourhood of Lilongs that was being systematically demolished.

The street pattern of the neighbourhood was a clever example of dense urban living – rows of houses, each with a front and a rear courtyard, facing a street on one side and a lane on the other, allowing for cross-ventilation to moderate the humid climate. We were invited inside one of the houses that was once the home of a merchant family but was now carved into many small rooms for separate families, who all shared one kitchen and a communal bathroom. On an upper floor we visited an elderly couple and had tea. All the possessions they once had in their rural village home were crammed into one room. They proudly showed us photos of their daughters, all living in the

United States, one of them a violinist with the San Francisco Symphony.

The husband took us up to the roof deck to show us the signboard from his former business – a sign-maker's shop – that had been demolished recently. He then pointed to one of the high-rise apartment buildings not far away, just visible in the smog, where he and his wife were expected to move shortly to take up residence in an apartment they had to purchase before their Lilong house would be demolished.

The next day we travelled to Pudong, the emerging office and trade centre, just barely visible through the smog across the Huangpu River from the Bund, the historic waterfront of Shanghai. The Pearl Tower stood out for its audacious design: a slender tower topped by a sphere. The plastic replica I brought home eventually made the rounds of several Secret Santa offerings amongst my architectural colleagues back in Vancouver.

I have scant interest in seeing what has become of Shanghai today. The writing was already on the wall twenty years ago, with glitzy international brand names ostentatiously sprouting up along historic Nanjing Avenue. As Chen Yi pointed out beggars on the Bund, back then still something new for this emerging empire, I realized that this was a place in a confused state of transition.

Considering the advancement of China on the world stage today, it is astonishing that a mere two decades ago, Canada and other Western nations like Norway and France were asked to pitch in and help bring Xi'an into the twenty-first century. Now, a fifth of the way through the twenty-first century, China leads the world in high-speed rail lines and other astonishing achievements of infrastructure and engineering.

The report I co-wrote with Larry Beasley and Louise Morris about the project received an honour award from the Canadian Institute of Planning. I can only hope that its methodology and recommendations have been implemented.

(•◆•)

One of the joys of travel for me is enjoying the local food, and in Xi'an the food was outstanding. We went to food stalls on the street and restaurants that were both tiny and grand. There were modern food courts where orders were tallied on chip cards and the food eaten sitting at plastic tables. We had excellent stretched noodles from street vendors, very good scallion cakes, crepe purses filled with mushrooms, and once a whole steamed fish topped with a spicy soy, ginger, garlic and jalapeno sauce. When someone felt under the weather, hot Coke with grated ginger was prescribed.

According to the Chinese zodiac, I was born in the year of the horse. On the wall at home is a print of a Chinese warrior on a chestnut-coloured horse, rearing dramatically. I had haggled with Peter for its purchase, picking it out from the wares he displayed on the steps outside the Bell Tower

Hotel. The framing cost considerably more than the print, and there are likely thousands sold to tourists across China. But I like it as a lovely souvenir of my work in Xi'an, and as both a reminder of China's past and an omen of the wariness I felt for its future.

(•)

CASTLE HOWARDS END

T HE HOUSE WAS dark, as usual, when I returned from rowing practice one night. My housemate Frank was obsessed with turning off (indeed unplugging) any sources of electricity, especially the telly, when not in use. But there was an odd odour when I opened the door – rather sweet and acrid – and I assumed it was the smell of Frank's supper of sweet-and-sour pork, which he ate regularly as it was cheap. He kept the leftovers in *his* frying pan in *his* refrigerator for his next meal.

I went into the drab kitchen, which looked like those in the movies *Little Voice* and *Billy Elliot* – the walls lined with treacherous wiring – to boil water for the day's washing up. Hot water had not flowed from the kitchen tap in fifteen years. My routine was to boil a large pot of water so I could wash all the day's dishes, plus some extra water to fill a stainless steel thermos I could use to shave with the next morning. All to avoid using the very frightening electric immersion heater rigged to the showerhead. That's where Frank shaved.

I was about to light the hob when I realized the range was still on. The smell was gas – one match would have exploded the south end of a row of Victorian terrace houses on Howard Street in York.

(◆◆◆)

Just two months after travelling to Xi'an, I was off to York to spend the summer of 1998 writing my master's thesis at King's Manor, the University of York's centre for archaeology, housed in a splendid fifteenth-century stone building. This would complete my master's degree in architectural conservation that had begun fourteen years earlier while attending ICCROM in Rome. ICCROM had an arrangement with the University of York to apply credit for the studies in Rome towards a thesis and master's degree at York.

With my architectural practice on hold and my bags packed, including my Rocky Mountain bike, Aldo Rossi *conica* Alessi espresso pot and a new laptop, I set out on my journey: a BA flight to London, then a connection to Manchester, followed by a train trip, burdened with luggage, to York, where I collapsed in slumber at a bed and breakfast. Without having time to find a place to live in York, two days later it was back to the Manchester airport for a flight to Prague with my King's Manor class for a week-long study trip.

During that time in the Czech Republic I had the chance to meet the

twenty or so other students in the architectural conservation program, some of whom were fellow architects. Others were archaeologists and one was a sculptor. Most were British, one was from India and there was a fellow Canadian. I had been to Prague two years earlier returning from a conference in Slovakia, but on this trip we were led to little-known places, and I discovered the genius of the early twentieth-century architect Josef Plečnik and his modern work at Prague Castle.

The study trip to Prague helped me crystalize the topic for my thesis. As an architect and heritage planner, I had confronted the challenge of getting old and new buildings to coexist, and Plečnik's work, along with the copper watchtowers in Copenhagen (described in "Tordenskjoldsgade"), formed the germ of my thesis: how modern buildings can fit into historic places.

On my return to York, I embarked on my research with the idea that, by analyzing modernist buildings in historic settings, I could develop a relatively objective methodology to assess whether a new building was compatible with, yet distinguishable from, its surroundings so that new and old were not confused, and the new building was clearly seen as a product of its time.

(•◆•)

But first I had to find a place to live. When I returned to York from Prague I had been posted to a student residence on the modern campus of the university on the outskirts of York. I shared a house – and one bathroom – with ten students two decades my junior. The kitchen was a mess, with dishes always stacked in the sink. Of course I washed them all before making myself coffee every morning in my Alessi espresso pot. That stay lasted exactly one week before I set out to find something better.

After scouring the local realty offices for a summer rental, I stumbled upon a room in a Victorian terrace house at the end of Howard Street. It seemed fine when I first saw it – a two-storey brick building, a bit sooty and tired but with a bay window and buddleia bush in front and a walled courtyard in the rear. Mrs. Cooper promised a new television for my arrival, and there was a washing machine in the kitchen. The location was just outside the walls of York City, a short walk to the River Ouse and close to the Barbican Leisure Centre with its swimming pool.

And I met Frank.

What I didn't notice on my first visit was the books on the dining room shelves. Next to *A Year in Provence* sat copies of *Evil Women, Unsolved Murder Mysteries* and a dozen or so volumes with similarly sinister titles. The dining room was notable for its drab gray wallpaper, worn brown-patterned carpet and a bare light bulb, though it was brightened by a large sash window. Frank asked me if I liked his pictures, several of which hung, unframed, on the walls. They were a note of bright hyperrealism, painted on slightly warping hardboard. Over the fireplace hung a sterile scene of rows of low-rise council flats, entirely devoid of life. A giant white hairbrush was conspicuously lying atop the buildings. Another scene was a sylvan landscape of Royal Mail postboxes arranged like tombstones. And next to the kitchen door was a meticulously rendered female nude with roses covering her face and breasts.

As I gazed out the window to the paved courtyard, I began to worry that I had made a grave mistake in moving to 25 Howard Street. Why was the room I had just taken vacant? Could the previous tenant be buried beneath the concrete slabs in the yard? Was this the site of another North Yorkshire murder mystery? I now faced the prospect of spending the better part of four months shoehorned into a tiny room – seven feet by ten feet

– with a shared bathroom and kitchen in a house with two other men I did not know.

It didn't take long for James Ashby, the fellow Canadian architect studying at York, to coin the term "Castle Howards End" for my summer lodgings. That was his portmanteau of British literature, blending the celebrated Castle Howard – located near York and used as Brideshead in the BBC series of Evelyn Waugh's *Brideshead Revisited* – with E.M. Forster's *Howards End*. Once quipped, the name stuck.

In cinematic terms, the place could not have been farther from the magnificence of Castle Howard or the charm of Howards End. Nor was it anything like the rose-covered cottage I was certain I would find that summer – a summer-holiday sublet from a university professor perhaps. Before leaving Vancouver I had pictured myself cycling happily around York on my bike, black robes flowing behind me, spending leisurely hours perusing leather-bound books in the King's Manor library, quaffing pints in the pub and rowing on the River Ouse. (This latter did become a reality when I joined the York City Rowing Club.)

It was only on move-in day that I discovered the reality of the frugal house rules from Frank. He told me that while there was a hot water tank in the house, it had not been turned on in fifteen years. I resigned myself to regular visits to the leisure centre for hot showers.

Even more peculiar was the arrangement with British Telecom. The only telephone in the house, on a tiny table in the upstairs hall, had a "BT low-user" rate, meaning that only incoming calls could be received to keep the rate rock-bottom. Any outgoing calls would send the bill skyrocketing. Frank's solution was to make phone calls from the red phone booth at the end of the street, something he had been doing for fifteen years. As my research meant that I had to use the phone line for Internet access, I was not too popular when the BT bill arrived. I ended up paying the entire bill for the summer.

I soon realized that Frank was on welfare and spent most of his time at the house. Mrs. Cooper's boast that he was a teacher at the posh Bootham School was a bit of a stretch, as it turned out he taught squash there once a week. His beloved motorcycle occupied pride of place in the courtyard and had a perennial "L" plate (for learner) as he could not afford to get it properly licensed. He was predictable in regularly blaming his lot in life on Lady Thatcher. Asked if he had ever been to London, something I did on a weekly basis and just two hours by train from York, he replied, "Why would I want to go there?" I had no retort.

The kitchen had a separate small fridge for Frank's food, and a few pans and dishes for his use alone. The washing machine was a godsend – it blessedly heated its own water, so I was able to keep my clothes clean. However, drying them in the damp house, or strung on the line in the courtyard in the dreary summer weather, was another matter. Clothes left out to dry in the morning were usually soaked after the inevitable rain shower during the day by the time I returned home in the evening.

Our domestic accord was challenged frequently. Mostly Frank and I steered clear of each other. Chris, the third housemate, was said to be a roaming BBC radio reporter. I met him only once.

After the gas incident, my Dorset friends the Hodginses made Lower Holt Farm available whenever I needed an escape. But I maintained my shabby digs on Howard Street for the duration of the summer and kept BT well funded and the British rail system busy with my comings and goings from York

(◆◆◆)

Researching my thesis topic, "Modernism in Context", went something like this: 1. Identify the problem; 2. Define "modernism"; 3. Figure out what "context" means; 4. Review literature about design guidelines for historic areas around the world; 5. Make a list of the buildings for case studies; 6. Develop a methodology for figuring out why some new buildings fit better than others in an historic context. Finally, rate the buildings as per my "fit" criteria and come up with a conclusion. This all had to be accomplished over the course of four months.

The time frame for my study was the Modern Movement from the late 1920s to the mid-1960s. I focussed on British buildings and compared them with Scandinavian ones, Danish in particular, as I was familiar with Denmark's modern buildings and there was a strong Scandinavian influence in the post-World War II rebuilding of England, especially academic

buildings. It happened that one of the most beautiful modern buildings in England, Oxford's St. Catherine's College, was designed by the Danish architect Arne Jacobsen.

I narrowed the scope of my research to four building types: academic, commercial, institutional or public, and multi-family residential. I left out single-family houses and religious buildings because they are often idiosyncratic or experimental, intended to stand out and not fit in. Next, I started researching books and journals and noting buildings that might be candidates for inclusion. I had quite a long list in the end, well over one hundred to review and vowed to see most of them in person.

My travels that summer in search of candidate buildings took me to Brighton, Cambridge, Dorchester, Durham, London, Norfolk and Oxford. Farther afield, my travels included Aarhus, Copenhagen, Nancy and Prague. Staying in York was not that important, and the research resources there were rather limited anyway. Lower Holt Farm became my regular escape where I would hammer away on the laptop to finish my thesis.

In early June I travelled to Copenhagen and with the help of Bente Lange looked for buildings. Bente also arranged for me to travel to Aarhus to see Arne Jacobsen's city hall and Kay Fisker's university campus. Those buildings made their way into my thesis.

(◆♦◆)

Back in England, my search for buildings continued. The university campuses of Cambridge and Oxford were ripe fodder for my work, as each city had a distinct historic architectural language and many buildings that had been added in the twentieth century. On a single day in Cambridge I had a guided tour with the architect Shawn Kholoucy.[1] He showed me seventeen clearly modern buildings of the mid-twentieth century in the hallowed context of historic Cambridge, designed by the likes of Powell & Moya, Edward Cullinan, Edwin Lutyens, David Roberts, Denys Lasdun, G.G. Scott, Leslie Martin, Colin St. John Wilson, Stirling & Gowan, Norman Foster, Hugh Casson & Neville Conder, the Cambridge Design Group, Henning Larsen and Quinlan Terry. It was a whirlwind day and a who's who of modernism.

Two days later I was in London, seeing five more modern buildings with the historian Alan Powers as my guide.[2] The following day I was in

---

1 I met Shawn at ICCROM in Rome in 1984. He is an expert in the conservation of British historic buildings and is closely involved with the SPAB – the Society for the Protection of Ancient Buildings. He was helpful to connect me with experts in the field of British modernism, including Alan Powers.
2 Alan has written many books on British modernism including *Bauhaus Goes West*.

Oxford to see another fourteen modern university buildings. Of those thir-ty-six buildings, fourteen were included in my thesis. It was a lot to digest.

One of the curious things about studying in Britain was navigating the library system. King's Manor had a respectable library and efficient, if not overly helpful staff. My first question was how the books were organized, as I had trouble finding some on the shelves. I learned that books were not catalogued by the Dewey Decimal System but by the slightly different Universal Decimal System.[3] Oversized books, including one I was hunting for, were called quartos (or perhaps they were folios), and these were all grouped together on the taller bottom shelves, not necessarily near their companions by topic or author. When I discovered that King's Manor did not have a copy of *Genius Loci*, the librarian ordered it by inter-library loan. After a six-week wait, and only after inquiring where it had come from, did the librarian confess that it was housed in the main British Library repository in Leeds, a twenty-minute train ride away from York. I could have gone there and picked it up myself.

---

3 The entire collection of over 7,500 books has since been re-catalogued to the Dewey system.

Don't get me wrong, York is a fascinating historic city, filled with important sites: the Minster, the walls, the Shambles, the Railway Museum and the Viking museum.[4] Yorkshire is beautiful, noted for its charming villages, hills and dales, coastline, grand country houses and remnants of centuries of habitation. The county even has famous puddings and terriers named after it. David Hockney hails from Yorkshire, and there is a museum of his art in the nineteenth-century company town of Saltaire. The fictitious Downton Abbey is set in the real Yorkshire. Many Ontario cities are named after places in Yorkshire – Scarborough, Whitby and Malton, for example. Toronto was originally called York. But York is also filled with tourists and their buses, and it sometimes felt like Ye Olde Yorke-on-the-Ouse.

Some of the frustrations of living and studying at York were offset by a very convivial circle of friends I met that summer. I bonded with my fellow Canadian James Ashby, who was writing his thesis on the historic use of aluminum (or as they say in England, "aluminium"). And one of the locals in the program and his partner, a docent at York Minster, also became friends. We made excursions to the countryside and the seaside, and to explore places in Yorkshire such as Fountains Abbey, Scarborough and Knaresborough. We celebrated the summer solstice with a chilly picnic atop Sutton Bank overlooking the vast, rolling countryside. My favourite diversion was Harrogate, an elegant spa town filled with handsome Georgian buildings and gardens just a short train ride from York. I found the remarkable Turkish Baths on one visit and returned several times to relish its high-Victorian architecture, tile-clad steam rooms and pools of hot and cold water. It was the perfect antidote to the cold-water digs in my house at the end of Howard Street.

(•♦•)

Hitting a roadblock in writing my thesis, I escaped to the Netherlands for a week of partying, enjoying Dutch hospitality and participation in the triathlon at the Gay Games. I travelled from York to Hull by train with my bicycle and its panniers packed with all my gear. When I boarded the

---

4 York is derived from the Danish *Jorek*.

overnight ferry for Rotterdam, my bike got a big red R sticker,[5] a souvenir I cherish. Arriving the next morning I was met by Robert, the partner of my DOCOMOMO colleague Wessel de Jonge.[6] We drove to their home in Rotterdam, where I stayed for a few days, touring the city. Rotterdam has a remarkable mix of pre-World War II buildings, some in a distinctive Dutch brick Rationalist style that fortunately survived the destruction of the war, along with a wealth of fine modernist buildings erected since then. Amsterdam, site of the Gay Games, was just a short train ride away.

The triathlon was held in Amsterdamse Bos, an English-style park on the edge of the city with a watercourse that dated from the world rowing championships in 1977. The first leg of the triathlon was the swim. Jumping into the sludgy, slimy water was a shock – I don't think the water had been cleaned since the rowing meet – and it took a while to adjust to the tightness of my wetsuit,[7] but I managed to complete the 1,500-metre swim. The second leg of the race was cycling a forty-kilometre bike course which snaked through the wooded park. Although I was at somewhat of a disadvantage having a mountain bike and not a proper road or triathlon bike, I managed to hold my own, even passing others with fancier bikes. I plodded along for the final ten-kilometre run and was happy to finish with a decent time. After a night celebrating with my fellow Vancouverites (and perhaps peeing in a canal after quaffing too much Heineken and *genever*), it was back to York and back to to my thesis.

(•◆•)

One of the highlights of academic life in England, if only for a summer, was a series of symposia on conservation by noted scholars on topics as diverse as the restoration of Windsor Castle after the fire of 1992, the chairs of Charles Rennie Mackintosh, the mosaic tiles of St. Paul's Cathedral and the concrete of the 1950s Centre Point tower in London, which became a Grade II listed building in 1995. We also had visits to remarkable houses

---

5 I have the same bike, now twenty-seven years old and the R sticker has just recently faded away.

6 Wessel was the founder of DOCOMOMO, the international NGO championing the DOcumentation and COnservation of MOdern MOvement architecture. I later established a B.C. chapter of DOCOMOMO and invited Wessel to give a talk in Vancouver.

7 Friends from Vancouver came to participate in the Games, and they brought my wetsuit.

and gardens at Castle Howard, Bishopsbarns, Burton Agnes and especially Ebberston Hall. Our King's Manor group had been invited to spend an evening at the latter, in the house designed by the celebrated Scottish architect Colen Campbell in 1718.[8]

The elegant Ebberston Hall is located in a secluded dale, its proportions spare but perfect. A pair of tall sash windows in the plain stone façade flank a central portico atop a flight of stone steps. A balustrade lines the top of the symmetrical façade, a little like a child's picture of a house drawn by one versed in the language of Andrea Palladio. Or a tiny version, cast in lead, would be a perfect token for a house in an 18th century version of Monopoly.

The austere front betrays a more open rear façade with a splendid recessed loggia which overlooked a once-grand water garden set in the Yorkshire dale. The perfect idyll for William Thompson and his mistress, it was owned in 1998 by the wonderfully named West de Wend-Fenton. No doubt my fondness for the symmetry of Ebberston harks back to that lovely Georgian house at 24 Rosebery Place which I recall from my childhood in St. Thomas.

(•◆•)

There was a mad dash in late August to complete my thesis – three hardbound copies of ninety-five pages, including three appendices and a six-page bibliography, were printed, bound in Leeds – and submit it to the thesis committee in preparation for their adjudication. What I thought was to be a "viva", an oral defence, turned out to be a critique, and it was less than enthusiastic. It seems that as someone from "the colonies", I had chosen a topic – British modernism – that was a bit too close to home for my thesis readers. A little miffed by the lukewarm response to my research, but with my MA secured, I packed up to leave York for good. But before returning to Vancouver I had another trip to Scandinavia to look forward to.

In early September I met my brother Paul in London then we were off to Copenhagen, where we spent a few days with Bente Lange. Then we

---

8 Campbell is perhaps better known for his neo-Palladian designs at Stourhead in Wiltshire and Burlington House in London.

took our bikes on an overnight ferry to Bornholm so we could circumnavigate the island. On my return I travelled to the DOCOMOMO conference in Stockholm to present a paper titled "Losses and Legacies: Vancouver's Burrard Street". In addition to a memorable reception at Gio Ponti's Italian Cultural Centre (1954), where we sipped cocktails while lounging on Ponti's swish furnishings, I had the chance to see some of the key works of the twentieth century that I had referred to in my thesis, including Ragnar Osberg's city hall (1923) and Gunnar Asplund's library (1928). I also saw Asplund's and Sigurd Lewerentz's Woodland Cemetery (1917–40), the second twentieth-century site on UNESCO's World Heritage list.

(• ◆ •)

That summer based in York was marked by both the trials and the joys of living, travelling and studying abroad, at a time when a pound sterling cost $2.75 Canadian. I have a hardbound thesis that has aided my work since then, and friends I met that summer, especially James Ashby, made the experience even more memorable. Reading James's thesis on "aluminium",

I learned that the apex of the Washington Monument (1884) is a nine-inch-high pyramid made from a solid block of aluminum. Who knew that aluminum was once as precious as gold?

(⋅)

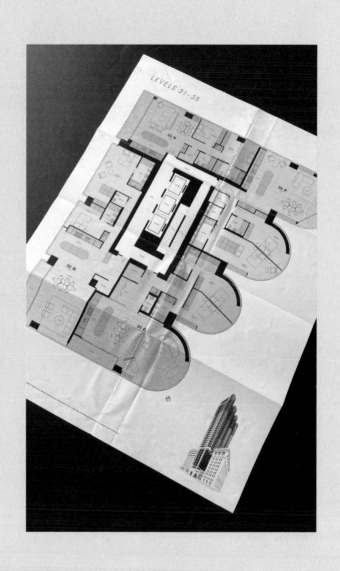

JH3403

Bob Ledingham and I were just curious to see the sales centre, having no serious interest in purchasing a pre-sale condominium. But the design pedigree was impressive.

The sculpted tower with curved glass bays stepping back from West Hastings Street in downtown Vancouver displayed the skill of the British architectural firm Foster + Partners, one of the best in the world. It was 2006 and this was their first residential building in Canada – and I was working on the project as the consulting heritage architect. The design, materials and detailing even impressed Bob who had consulted on the interiors of many high-end condos in Vancouver. By the end of the visit, we had put a deposit on suite 3403, high up in Jameson House.

For much of my career over four decades in Vancouver, I have been involved with heritage conservation, sometimes as the lead architect, but more often as the heritage consultant to a larger firm. Many of these

projects have have been honoured with awards, but Jameson House stands out for its exceptional blending of respect for heritage fabric with very accomplished modern design. The professionalism, skill, diligent process and imagination of the Foster team in fitting a mixed-use high-rise tower on a small site, including not one but two small heritage buildings, was impressive.

The site was a four-lot parcel, just thirty-two metres wide, in the financial hub of downtown Vancouver, two blocks from the harbour. The two small heritage buildings were sandwiched mid-block between the twelve-storey presence of the heritage landmark Credit Foncier building (1912) and a more mundane office building of the same height from the 1970s. One of the heritage buildings was the Ceperley Rounsfell building, a handsome two-storey Georgian Revival headquarters built for a mortgage company in 1921. Its interior originally boasted a splendid skylit double-height central area which had long been shuttered by the insertion of a subsequent floor level. Next door was the glazed terra cotta façade of the Royal Financial building dating from 1926, which was later converted to the headquarters of the BC and Yukon Chamber of Mines.

The tight, mid-block site needed a careful design to integrate the heritage buildings into what would become a thirty-six–storey office and

residential tower. That is where the skill of Foster + Partners came into play. They had teamed with Walter Francl's architectural firm in Vancouver, and I happened to share office space with Walter and his team so it was a smooth working relationship guiding the heritage conservation work as the tower development evolved. The team from London would come regularly to work with us in Francl's building.[1]

Foster's team worked through at least twelve iterations of various tower configurations and shapes, conscious of the environmental impact as well as the urban fit of the small heritage buildings that occupied half the site. Substantial cantilevers were involved, and structural and wind studies narrowed down the options to one that had a twelve-storey slim

1 I was given a tour of Foster's office overlooking the Thames on one of my visits to London.

office tower – aligning with the neighbouring buildings – and twenty-three storeys of condominium apartments hovering above. The distinctive half-round scalloped bays were a counterpoint to the solidity of the base, evoking the idea of clouds hovering above the heritage buildings. A high-tech Swiss-engineered elevator-driven parking system solved the problem of building a parkade on such a tight site – a conventional spiral ramp system would have gone nine levels underground.

To conserve the Ceperley building required an extraordinary structural solution to hang the building from massive steel trusses while the underground parking vault was excavated. The entire building was kept intact and *in situ* except for the terrazzo floor, which was replicated when the building was completed. The interior space, returned to its original double height with the historic skylight renewed, was complemented by sleek new staircases to the mezzanines.

Then things got complicated.

(•♦•)

First there was the financial meltdown in the fall of 2008. The financing for Jameson House fell through, and there was a serious concern that the project would go bankrupt. With fellow pre-sale purchasers, we balked and filed a lawsuit to cancel our contracts and retrieve our deposits. The judge disagreed. So we had no choice but to "complete" the purchase and own the unit. Fortunately, the project was rescued by an experienced developer – Bosa – who did an admirable job of finishing the project true to the Foster + Partners specifications.

Then we learned that the developer had approval from the city for an additional floor without changing the overall height of the building. They did this by shrinking the ceiling height of the lower thirty-four floors to create a new level thirty-five, one above us. We were no longer the sub-penthouse but the sub-sub-penthouse. With no choice in the matter, and at least pleased by the finished product, we moved in to give condo living a try.

The attention to design and detail of the condo suites was impressive. Smooth limestone floors which had embedded heating and cooling

coils extended, flush, to the broad east-facing terrace, a simple detail but complex to execute structurally without creating a thermal bridge from the outside to the interior. Our suite had recessed baseboards, a beautiful minimalist kitchen boasting an island with custom hydraulic countertops, and slick back-painted glass panels in the bathrooms. Bob and I decided that we would eventually sell the Barber House, have a pied-à-terre at Jameson House and spend more time at our country place, Estergreen.

We learned that there are certain advantages to living downtown, high up in the air. From our balcony we looked out over Burrard Inlet and downtown Vancouver, and I could see some of the buildings I had worked on, including the Hotel Georgia and the Architecture Centre.

An amenity with condo ownership was membership in a private club across the street and use of its twenty-five-metre lap pool. Sunday nights we would treat friends to the club's roast beef and Yorkshire pudding dinner, then decamp to the media room at Jameson House to watch *Downton Abbey*. There was a tiny bar nearby, just off the lobby of the old Stock Exchange Building, where we enjoyed Friday night buck-a-shuck oysters and a proper martini or two. We held a "Christmas-in-the-Clouds" cocktail party where our friend Juliette Cavazzi,[2] something of a legend in Canadian television as "Our Pet Juliette", held court and recounted stories of her show business career.

But as nice as it was, the 1,200-square-foot condo was rather too small for us, and we felt like nomads living in a hotel. As well, there was a proposal to build a massive office tower atop the old Stock Exchange Building across the lane, just twenty-eight feet from our bedroom window. Our favourite oyster bar was going to be history.

With Bob's health failing, we decided to sell. We accepted the only offer we got (for essentially our purchase price) and moved back to the Barber House. As I noted at the outset of *Address Book*, I never did meet Lord Foster but was honoured to work with his firm.

---

2 She hosted *Juliette*, a variety show that aired on CBC-TV from 1956 to 1966, right after *Hockey Night in Canada*.

(♦)

ORCHARD BEACH, MONTEZUMA, STRATFORD

AUNT JEAN'S ARRIVAL at 12 Rosebery Place in 1961 in her silver 1956 Jaguar XK140 convertible caused quite a stir. It had bright yellow Land of Enchantment plates, and black smoke spewed from the exhaust. She had driven for three days from Montezuma, New Mexico, to her cottage at Orchard Beach in Port Stanley, Ontario, with a stop in St. Thomas to say hello and have a beer before the final nine-mile trip down to "Port". My father, who never drank, would have bought a bottle or two of beer for her arrival.

While I have never lived at her Orchard Beach cottage or her winter home in Montezuma, they are the two homes of my aunt Jean, who was a very influential person in my life. They relate to my Ontario roots and my eventual move, decades later, to Stratford, Ontario, to create "seven&nine".

She introduced me to the Stratford Festival and piqued my interest in ultimately retiring there.

(•♦•)

Mary Jean Johnson was my father's older sister and by any measure a remarkable woman. Widowed in World War II and remarried after the war, for most of her adult life she summered May through August in an old wooden cottage at Orchard Beach on the shores of Lake Erie. She was joined by her daughter, my cousin Leslie, (who was exactly my age) and a large dog (first Sheba, the giant Newfoundland, and later Rupert, the German shepherd). The rest of the year she taught romance languages at Highlands University in Las Vegas, New Mexico, and lived in one of a tiny cluster of adobe houses in Montezuma, just up the road from the old Hot Springs Hotel, high in the pine forests of the Sangre de Cristo Mountains. Her husband, Bill Johnson (Uncle Swede to us), usually stayed in New Mexico, where the dry climate suited his allergies more than the humidity of Ontario summers.

Aunt Jean's cottage sat high up on a hill overlooking the lake. The cottage was old, dating from 1901, one of many built in Port Stanley in the late nineteenth and early twentieth centuries when it was a pleasure ground of summer activity. Growing up, my father's family would spend summers at their family cottage in Port Stanley, on another beach farther west. It was just nine miles south of their turreted house at 100 Wellington Street in St. Thomas.

Situated at the centre of the north shore of Lake Erie, Port Stanley was a thriving port, lake fishery and summer resort due to its splendid sandy Main Beach. The Stork Club – once the largest dance hall in Ontario – graced the boardwalk along the beach where the likes of Count Basie, Glenn Miller, Duke Ellington, Guy Lombardo, Louis Armstrong and Benny Goodman played. Also along the boardwalk was Mackie's, where orangeade and steamed hot dogs have been famous since 1911. The L&PS Railway ran from London through St. Thomas, to Port Stanley.

The cottage was a modest single-storey building clad in white-painted wood siding with green trim and a red asphalt-shingled hipped roof. It sat

high up on a steep slope set back a block from the lake. Like most Ontario cottages, it was a summer seasonal home with no insulation. In fact, the interior walls were just the exposed studs of the exterior framing, painted white. There was a large stone fireplace, and a series of rambling additions included bedrooms, a low-ceilinged kitchen and an outdoor shower. Some of the windows slid down into pockets below the sill.

Aunt Jean would spend her summers in Port Stanley stationed in her favourite wicker chair on the screened porch, binoculars by her side, overseeing the view of Lake Erie. She smoked endlessly, had a can of Labatt's 50 or IPA always at hand and was a fiend for contract bridge, birdwatching and cryptic crosswords. She subscribed to the *Manchester Guardian* to have the weekly grid-less cryptic crossword puzzle mailed to her. She usually nailed it.

Every day she would walk down to the beach for a morning swim, despite the fact that during much of the 1960s and 70s Lake Erie's water could generously be described as murky. Shore erosion made the water even siltier. Some summers she would take off for a tour of Europe with cousin Leslie.[1] In spite of the U.S. boycott, Aunt Jean travelled to the Moscow Olympics in 1980. I was very impressed by her resolve.

Rain or shine, Sunday meals that Aunt Jean hosted with my family were taken at the big black-painted dining table on the screened porch. The best meal was a feast of local yellow perch. The fillets were dredged in flour, then fried in oil and served with boiled potatoes, platters of peaches-and-cream

---

1 Leslie was the same age as I, and one year she was sent to school in Switzerland. She and Aunt Jean travelled there on the SS *France*. I was very jealous.

corn, sliced tomatoes sprinkled with sugar (for some reason, sugaring local beefsteak tomatoes was a custom in my family) and cucumbers soaked in vinegar. Fried yellow perch remains one of my favourite meals. After dinner we would play card games on the table – Pounce, Bird-O and, my favourite, Mille Bornes. That game of road trips through France, marked by the "bornes" (stone roadside distance markers), probably sparked my interest in travel.

(•♦•)

One March, on spring break from high school, my brother Peter and I flew to New Mexico to visit Aunt Jean in Montezuma. Our flight itinerary would not be possible today. From London (the one in Ontario) to Cleveland to Denver and Albuquerque, then a long drive past Santa Fe to her adobe house near Las Vegas, above the Hot Springs Hotel. The hotel was a fairy-tale Victorian pile – not unlike the Banff Springs Hotel – built in 1886 and reached by the Atchison, Topeka and Santa Fe Railway. The building was designed by the Chicago firm of Burnham and Root to take advantage of its spectacular mountain location next to the historic hot springs. A few adobe homes had been built close by, and that is where Aunt Jean lived. On our first visit there, the hotel was derelict, and when cousin Leslie gave us a tour, it seemed rather creepy, like the hotel in *The Shining*. Since then it has been rehabilitated as the United World College's American campus, named after Armand Hammer.

For a teenager who, until then, had never been outside Canada, to visit Aunt Jean at her exotic home was an eye-opener in so many ways. She had a cultured and eccentric circle of academic friends who enjoyed the spaciousness and energy of the place, much as other artists like Georgia O'Keeffe had. At one Sunday brunch I had my first Bloody Mary.

We toured Navajo and old U.S. military fort sites. We went to Taos, with its historic Pueblo buildings, visited Santa Fe and dined at La Fonda. We drove on the serpentine roads in the pine-forested mountains in one of Uncle Swede's vintage sports cars – a Porsche, I think – while he double-clutched. I had never even heard of double clutching before.

Most memorable was a visit to the hacienda of Aunt Jean's friend Richard Pritzlaff, a flamboyant figure from a wealthy family in Wisconsin. Richard had studied architecture and landscape architecture at UC Berkeley, and he was now breeding Arabian horses on the 3,300-acre Rancho San Ignacio he had established in northern New Mexico in the 1940s. His house was filled with Chinese antiques, and there were peacocks in the portal. This was where I had my first Bellini, properly made with white peach juice and *prosecco*. It opened my eyes to the world beyond the confines of St. Thomas.

(•♦•)

As she always returned to New Mexico before my late-September birthday, Aunt Jean would treat me to an early celebration with a trip to see a play at the Stratford Shakespearean Festival. The first time was in 1961 when I was eight years old. We made the hour's drive from St. Thomas to Stratford in her oil-burning Jaguar convertible, with cousin Leslie sitting on the transmission hump. We saw Gilbert and Sullivan's *Pirates of Penzance* at the Avon Theatre. Ever since that time I have been hooked on theatre, opera and arts in general, and Stratford, Ontario, in particular.

It was not until her death in 2007, when I was writing a "Lives Lived" tribute to Aunt Jean in the *Globe and Mail*, that I understood what a talented and gifted person she was. With degrees from the University of Western Ontario and University of Toronto, she went on to earn her PhD at the University of North Carolina at Chapel Hill. Her thesis was on "Comparative Indo-European Linguistics". I have no idea what that means.

In the balcony of Stratford's Festival Theatre (Aisle 5, Left, Row B, Seat 118) is an inscription that I sponsored in her honour. It reads "Dr. Jean Johnson – She opened my eyes to the wonders of the stage". Six decades after my first view of the stage at Stratford, I am returning there to live.

(♦)

seven&nine

A S ONE ARRIVES BY CAR from the west, the highway sign says "Welcome to Stratford, home of the Stratford Festival and the Ontario Pork Congress". Added to that mix of culture and agriculture is a legacy of both railway and furniture industries, a splendid park system, a vibrant downtown and streets lined with lovely Victorian buildings. It all makes Stratford, Ontario, one of the most beautiful small cities in Canada. I visited Stratford, about ninety kilometres (just over an hour's drive) from my hometown of St. Thomas, countless times in my youth for the theatre. Even while living in Vancouver for over four decades, I travelled to Stratford almost every year to take in the festival.

As a retired architect, I decided to move to Stratford with my husband, Franco, and establish an inn. Friends in Vancouver looked puzzled when I told them of my purchase of two properties in downtown Stratford, overlooking Lake Victoria. Why would you move to Ontario? Aren't the winters horrible? Don't you love the mountains and the ocean? Why choose Stratford over St. Thomas? Are you sure you want to be an innkeeper?

The reasons are many. All my brothers and their families live in Ontario. It is easier to get to Europe from Toronto's YYZ than from Vancouver's YVR. Stratford is far enough from Toronto (where the citizens think they live in the centre of the universe) to be distant but just a two-hour train ride away. There is history in Stratford, and splendid historic buildings as well as some good modern ones. The park system threads through the heart of the city and there is an outdoor swimming pool in summer months. The theatre and music offerings are outstanding and there is no shortage of very good food.

The needs of theatre-going and music-loving visitors have spurred a robust economy of good restaurants, coffee houses, markets, shopping and places to stay. Many actors, musicians, writers and artists have moved to Stratford, adding to the city's vitality.

Stratford is within a reasonable day's drive of three of the five Great Lakes. Located along the northern edge of the old Carolinian forest that once covered this area, the vegetation – mostly deciduous – tends to be a brighter yellow-green than the dark deep blue-green that marks the coniferous coverings of British Columbia. There are distinct changes of seasons, and the fall foliage is splendid in Ontario. Even in winter it can be beautiful, especially on a bright clear day when the countryside around Stratford is covered in snow and the stark shapes of the deciduous trees' dark brown branches contrast with the brilliant white of the snow.

(◆)

Stratford's location, almost dead centre in southwestern Ontario, is reflected in its unusual Y-shaped layout and its street names. Ontario Street stretches east, generally toward the lake of the same name, from its terminus at the handsome courthouse cleverly sited on axis with Stratford's broad main thoroughfare. Erie Street heads south, more or less in the direction of London and pointing to Lake Erie, while Huron Street takes you westward, directly to Goderich on Lake Huron.

The nexus of the three spokes is a public square in downtown, now a heritage conservation district. The Y street pattern gives rise to some

distinctive building shapes, exemplified in the Renaissance Revival Stratford city hall's hexagonal response to its triangular site.

Civic boosters in the early twentieth century battled railway interests who wanted to transform the old millpond along the Avon River for rail purposes. Instead, an impressive system of parks was created in close proximity to the centre of town. When the Grand Trunk Railway left town in the 1950s, the loss of this major industry helped spur citizens to create the Stratford Shakespearean Festival under the direction of England's Tyrone Guthrie. From its tent beginnings in 1953, the festival has grown to be North America's largest repertory theatre company, attracting 500,000 people to Stratford during the season which runs from May to November. Buildings and businesses related to the theatre, including a celebrated chef's school, have transformed the city.

As much as I admire the history and architecture of my hometown of St. Thomas, there is something more appealing about Stratford, even when it comes to their shared history of railroads. Despite St. Thomas's claim to be the "The Railway City", there is no longer any passenger service there, the tracks of the former New York Central Railway having been torn up and the railroad legacy diminished. At least a prominent trestle has been made into a kind of High Line park. While St. Thomas's splendid passenger station is still there, Stratford's more modest station still sees passenger train traffic.[1]

(•◆•)

Stratford is known for its collection of handsome Victorian buildings, but there are many buildings from the twentieth century that are worth noting. Many relate to the impact that the theatre festival has had, and I am working with the local architectural conservancy on a tour of "Modern Stratford". I purchased one of these modern buildings, the Tower House. It was designed by Brigitte Shim and Howard Sutcliffe twenty years ago and is listed on the tour. Tower House has been featured in many international publications. Shim–Sutcliffe Architects espouses critical regionalism and is among the very best firms in Canada, if not the world, according to critic Kenneth Frampton. The firm's RAIC Gold Medal in 2021 is testament to the principals' talent and standing in the field of architecture.

I first met Brigitte Shim when she, Bob Ledingham and I were on the jury for the Prairie Design Awards in 2005, when we spent a frigid February weekend in Regina deliberating over the submissions. My worries that Brigitte would be a formidable figure wrapped in black capes and dangerous jewelry were for naught. She was delightful – as well as

---

1 There are a pair of videos that tell the stories of how railways shaped these two cities better than I can here: *The Railways of St. Thomas-Elgin* and *Grand Trunk – A City Built on Steam* are well worth watching.

brilliant, a good teacher and a champion of historic houses, which she says need someone to look after them. Years later, when I had the chance to buy Tower House and the adjacent Rundles restaurant building, I was happy to be the new custodian of one of her buildings.

The Tower House is tall and narrow, only sixteen feet wide and sixteen hundred square feet in size, arranged on six levels around a central skylit atrium that makes it seem much larger. Its carefully placed windows

overlook the lake and focus the morning views east from the bedroom and the evening views west from the living room. The interior is meticulously detailed in cedar and fir, with bespoke metal railings and custom cabinetry. The entire east wall is concrete – eighteen feet high and sixty feet long – and it is shared with the former restaurant on the other side. The koi pond, framed in concrete, is flush with the kitchen countertop height. There are references to Tadao Ando, Carlo Scarpa and a bit of Alvar Aalto in the detailing, but all done in a site-specific way.

The former Rundles restaurant, connected to Tower House by that massive concrete wall, had been one of the best restaurants in Canada since its founding in the late 1970s by James Morris. The rear part of the building dates to an 1880s brick woodworking shop. In the late 1990s, Morris commissioned Shim–Sutcliffe to design a major renovation in which the dining room was expanded and a new bar was added, along with a front deck featuring a concrete fishpond.

(•♦•)

For many years, Bob and I stayed at Tower House while visiting Stratford. When Jim Morris decided to close Rundles and list both buildings for sale, I happened to be staying at Tower House and had dinner at Rundles on September 23, 2017, the restaurant's last day of service. It also happened to be my birthday. Jim knew of my interest in the buildings, but with Barber House still on the market, I hesitated to put in an offer. Someone eventually bought the properties, and I had forgotten about them until one day in February 2019 when Jim called me. His sale had fallen through, and the buildings were back on the market. That was the same day I got my one and only offer on the Barber House. I ended up buying both of Jim's properties and decided to retire with Franco to Stratford. The rest is history.

Well, just barely history, as three years later it is still not quite done. Because of the buildings' location in the downtown district of Stratford, the zoning does not allow purely residential use, although having a dwelling as part of an inn is allowed. So that is what I have developed, a small inn called seven&nine. Becoming an innkeeper was not something I had ever contemplated in my retirement, and I was certainly not up to having a bed and breakfast, or keen to make muffins every morning for guests. But I had done research on the Landmark Trust in the United Kingdom as a model for self-catered "holidays in historic places". I planned to keep the modern landmark Tower House as is and have the whole house available for guests to experience its design.

I struggled over a name for the inn but settled on the obvious, simply because the buildings are located at 7 and 9 Cobourg Street. I purchased all the original modernist furnishings that had been in Tower House – pieces designed by Le Corbusier, Frank Gehry and Mies van der Rohe. Works from my art collection, including pieces by Foster Eastman, Glenn Lewis, Clark McDougall, Graham Murdoch, Alan Switzer and Kathy Venter are now in Tower House.

As for the former Rundles building, it has taken on a new life as the hub of the seven&nine inn. On the main floor is the Lake Salon, a space for recitals and private dinners, graced with a vintage Yamaha concert grand piano, a large kitchen, an office and lounge. Upstairs there is a master suite with an *onsen*. Two rental guest suites have been added – the Garden Suite overlooks the courtyard, and upstairs is the Garret Studio with its own kitchen. Together with my friend Neil Ironside as the architect, we carved out a garage in the rear. For the interiors, I had the help of Sandrine Lejeune, a very talented designer who had worked for Bob Ledingham. The team at Belliveau Construction did an amazing job of repairing, adding and finishing the extensive overhaul of the building.

Overseeing an extensive renovation project during a pandemic and at a great distance has had its challenges. But the end result has exceeded my expectations. The next chapter of my career is about to start.

(•)

POST SCRIPT

This book is about the places where I have lived – and mostly had mailing addresses - and that shaped my career, yet there are many more places I have travelled that have also influenced my thinking about architecture, history, gardens, cities and food. How fortunate that travel is part of the job of an architect, to see and experience what is old and new.

While I do not talk about them in *Address Book*, the list of other influential places I have visited is extensive. I have been to all of Canada's ten provinces and three territories and attended conferences or given papers in Banff, Ottawa, Peterborough, Saint John, Toronto, Vancouver and Victoria. I have visited thirty-seven of the fifty states in the USA and attended conferences or given papers in Austin, Boston, Chicago, Denver, Miami, New Orleans, New York, Philadelphia, San Juan, San Francisco, Seattle and Spring Green. I have a fondness for Mexico, and while beach vacations in Puerto Vallarta are fine, I find Mexico City much more interesting. CDMX is one of the most vibrant cities in the world for culture, architecture and food. Two weeks in Cuba, hosted by a family, was an eye-opener. I have yet to venture to South America, but I hope that by working with Pablo Mandel on this book I will at last get to Buenos Aires.

Europe has been a draw ever since that first BOAC jumbo jet flight to London fifty years ago. I suspect it will continue to lure me back in my retirement years. So far I have explored the buildings, gardens and food of England, Scotland and Ireland and brought back ideas and reflections from each place. Not mentioned in *Address Book* are travels in Austria, Belgium, Finland, Germany, Greece, Monaco, the Netherlands, Norway, Portugal, Slovakia, Spain and Switzerland. I am not sure if Istanbul counts as Europe or Asia, but I have been there twice, once for a week at a post-Marmara earthquake UNESCO conference. I was mesmerized by the city and found the Bosporus fascinating.

So far Africa has been given short shrift, as I have only spent three weeks in Kenya and Tanzania on safaris and visiting with friends stationed there doing AIDS work in Nairobi. We spent a memorable Christmas in a stone farmhouse on the shores of Lake Naivasha, and Christmas Eve singing carols at the owners' Art Deco villa nearby. That night a hippo landed in their empty swimming pool. I also took a two-week road trip through Morocco with my L.A. friends, in the company of a devout but otherwise modern Muslim guide, a divorced single mother.

There have been just a few ventures to Asia, with two trips to Hong Kong and India (once to a yoga ashram in Rishikesh) and one to Sri Lanka, where I was taken by the work of Geoffrey Bawa and stayed at his home, Lunuganga. I have been to Thailand and the Philippines and spent a few weeks in Australia, including a visit to a remote sheep station where the sheep were nowhere to be seen. The work of the late Australian architect Kerry Hill has drawn me to his Aman lodges in Bhutan, where he nailed a modern interpretation of the local vernacular. Stunning too are his Aman hotels atop a high-rise tower in Tokyo and overlooking Ago Bay in Japan; in those places he understood the context and designed in his remarkably elegant aesthetic.

Many of those trips were in the company of Bob Ledingham, as his interior design projects required travelling to design marts, antique shops and trade shows in Chicago, London, Los Angeles, New York, and Paris. He designed the interiors of hotels in Vancouver and Whistler, so our travels would always include "research" with stays and visits at hotels old and new in each city, at least to have a martini at the bar. We both took inspiration from those trips.

Details of those visits are tucked away in the back of my mind or jotted down in my journals and itineraries. They might become a *Little Black Book* follow-up to *Address Book*. But it is the places where I settled for a time and lived – and people I met there – that have been most influential in my career.

(•♦•)

I was asked when I started writing this book "Who would want to read your memoir?" I am still not sure. I do not have any landmark buildings with my name on them. I will not be written about, except perhaps in connection to some of the buildings I have rehabilitated. Some of my articles and lectures may have given people reason to think about conservation. I am thrilled when friends and clients ask for travel tips – where to stay and where to eat. That the buildings I have worked on are still around and being put to good use is a proud legacy of my four-decade career. I hope that people will remember some of the meals I have prepared. I am proud to give jars of "Norma's Chili Sauce" as hostess gifts.

I think I am a forager, not a hunter, when it comes to planning a meal. And something similar as an architect. A hunter will decide to make a specific recipe and then source all the ingredients. A forager will take what's at hand and work around that to make a meal. That's what I do in the kitchen and in my design studio. I like the limitations of working with available ingredients, and I suppose my work with old buildings is similar. Working with what is already there instead of fretting about where to start is a relief. Being inspired by what has come before, working within a shell, adding to it and adapting to its architectural roots fascinates me. My portfolio is erratic in that regard, as I have worked on an eighteenth-century farmhouse in Dorset, a 1920s Moroccan house in Los Angeles, an Art Moderne house and several Craftsman and Tudor-style buildings in Vancouver, and on islands in British Columbia have rebuilt an historic timber frame house and designed a modern wooden one, none of which show a pattern of design or formula, as each is different.

I suppose my quest to answer the question of how new buildings fit with old started way back in my time on Vancouver's heritage advisory committee, when I was perplexed by how difficult it was for architects to design additions to old buildings. The easy, and very unsatisfying, approach was to copy the old, often literally. But what place does a mock Tudor house have in the twenty-first century? And how does a copy speak to being a product of its time?

So when I write about Rome, I see the layers and layers of history expressed in fragments of stone, in an ancient column or the outline of something centuries old but kept, added to and continuing to function today.

I look to the local context for inspiration and want keenly to see if what I do "fits in". I suppose that is the takeaway from my thesis "Modernism in Context". If I were to have a legacy I would hope that it would help people come to an understanding of how to look at new buildings in historic contexts and make decisions based on how they are compatible yet distinguishable and a product of their time. And be reversible should circumstances change. Just like the repair of the *lacunae* in the paintings I saw in the conservation labs at Le Louvre. Or that very visible bronze staple repair to the handle on an old English porcelain vegetable dish.

Architecture may be simply the alchemy of science and art with an overlay of creativity and good taste.

And in answer to the original question of why one might want to be an architect, I have this to reply. I cannot imagine another profession that would have offered me the chance to travel to interesting places, live in such fascinating places as Paris, London, Rome, York and Vancouver, meet lifelong friends and make a career of it.

These are the things that have shaped the career of this architect.

Robert Lemon
Vancouver, June 2022

(♦)

ACKNOWLEDGEMENTS

There are many people who must be thanked for their help with this book. For no reason other than my Virgo-on-the-cusp-of-Libra proclivities, I will thank them in alphabetical order.

James Ashby is at the top of the list, not just for reviewing a few early chapters and the final manuscript but also for coining the term "Castle Howards End". He was quick to see the humour in my tawdry lodgings in York. I thank him for his continued interest in the conservation of modern heritage.

When I telephoned Paul Baldwin, my grade-ten high school history teacher, in Ottawa recently, he had just returned from hiking, solo, a stretch of the Camino di Santiago. I was startled by his razor-sharp recall of things that happened decades ago in St. Thomas. Good teachers are invaluable, and he was one of the best.

The experience of studying at ICCROM led to many friendships in addition to Agnès Cailliau and Bente Lange. I count Shawn Kholucy among them, and when I was embarking on my master's thesis at York, his expertise and connections in conservation in the United Kingdom were enormously helpful. He linked me to experts in the field and guided me through Cambridge and Norfolk. I enjoyed staying with him at his splendidly named house "Three Trees, Cross Street, Hoxne, Eye, Suffolk," and we also shared a stay at Mackintosh's Hill House.

I thank Audrey McClellan for editing the first chapters, long before this became an actual book. And for looking at it again in its final form. She made sure the stories had both a beginning and an ending.

Joanne McInnis is a curator of the Nunavut collection, where the artefacts from the Dealy Island Archaeological Project are held, near Ottawa. She kindly opened up many of the items so I could see them. I know it was a monumental task so I thank you, Joanne, for the pleasure of seeing that tin of tripe and onions again.

Four women in Vancouver, all writers, have helped me along the way. Kerry McPhedran boosted my confidence when she reviewed early versions of my stories. Adele Weder was the sharp-tongued critic who was absolutely right to ask who would want to read my memoir. Thanks, Adele, for your frankness. Anicka Quinn of *Western Living* magazine kindly allowed portions of "Our Estergreen" to be used. Jan Whitford used her publishing experience to hone my resume, and later took pencil in hand to go over every word of what I thought was a final version of the manuscript. I thank her for ensuring it makes sense.

The Christopher Foundation was generous in helping fund this venture, and the Vancouver Heritage Foundation has helped with its launch.

Yosef Wosk was generous in helping bring this book to press. A lover of books, I was honoured to design the library in his historic house. I would also like to thank Brigitte Shim for introducing me to the team at ORO Editions.

It has been a pleasure working with Gordon Goff, Kirby Anderson, Meridith Murray and particularly the book designer Pablo Mandel. You have brought the words and pictures of the addresses where I have lived to the printed page.

Last but not least (and out of alphabetical order) is my husband, Franco Monfort, who has patiently watched and listened while I wrote *Address Book* and read the drafts to him.

(•)

A NOTE ON THE FONT

Book designer Pablo Mandel chose Adobe Minion Pro, an Adobe Original typeface designed by Robert Slimbach for Address Book. The first version of Minion was released in 1990. Minion Pro is inspired by classical typefaces of the late Renaissance, a period of elegant, beautiful, and highly readable type designs.

PHOTO CREDITS

All photos by the author except as listed below.

Back Cover: Franco Monfort

Rear Flap: Rohan Roy

p.4: Roger Brooks

p.6: Franco Monfort

p.12: Scott Studios, St. Thomas

p.28: Elgin County Archives

p.40: Neil Ironside

p.64: Architectural Association, London

p.90: Paul Larocque

p.95: Martin Tessler

p.96: Martin Tessler

p.102: Martin Tessler

p.130: Roger Brooks

p.137: Ross Lort drawing

p.146: Martin Knowles

p.149: Roger Brooks

p.150: Paul Joseph

p.157: Roger Brooks (top)

p.157 : Martin Knowles (bottom)

p.162: private collection

p.164: Malcolm Parry, Vancouver Sun

p.211: City of Vancouver Archives

p.241: Elgin County Archives

p.258: Franco Monfort

p.263: Franco Monfort

p.264: Rohan Roy

p.264: Governors' Palace Archives, New Mexico

REFERENCES

Architectural Conservancy of Ontario – Stratford/Perth. "Grand Trunk: A City Built on Steam." Stratford: Video. September 2021. https://www.tvo.org/video/documentaries/grand-trunk-a-city-built-on-steam

Baker, Mike (curator), and Paul Baldwin (essayist). *J. T. Findlay: Architect*. St. Thomas: Elgin County Museum catalogue of exhibit 17 September 2012 to 28 March 2013.

Cailliau, Agnès, Bente Lange and Robert Lemon. "Interventions in an historic building: Carlo Scarpa's work in Museo Castelvecchio in Verona. Rome, ICCROM, unpublished report for course in architectural conservation, 1984.

"Colour in the City" *Conference Brochure*. Vancouver: Simon Fraser University, February 1996.

"Conserving Architectural Terra Cotta" *Conference Brochure*. Vancouver: Simon Fraser University, February 1993.

Corneil, Carmen. "Architectural Specification for Carleton University School of Architecture." Calgary: Canadian Architectural Archives; Unpublished copy, January 1971.

David, Elizabeth. *An Omelette and a Glass of Wine*. New York: The Lyons Press, 1997.

Elgin Historical Society "Railways of St. Thomas Elgin." St. Thomas, Ontario: 2013. Video. https://www.youtube.com/watch?v=BcoT5B9uTug

Fitterman. Lisa, "Obituary: Designer Robert Ledingham Brightened Spaces – and Lives." Globe and Mail, 10 May 2013.

Friends of St. Thomas Public Library. *Memories of St. Thomas and Elgin; Volume One*. Aylmer Press, 1997.

Godley, Elizabeth. "Thoroughly Moderne". *Western Living Magazine*. Vancouver: January 1991, pp. 38–43.

Hett, Charles. "Archaeological Sites of the Canadian North: Their Preservation". *CCI The Journal of the Canadian Conservation Institute; Volume 3*. Ottawa: Canadian Conservation Institute, National Museums of Canada, 1979.

Hughes, Robert. *Rome*. London: Weidenfeld & Nicolson, 2011.

Janes, Robert R. "The preservation and Ethnohistory of a Frozen Historic Site in the Canadian Arctic." *Arctic. Vol.35, No 3*. Calgary: University of Calgary / Arctic Institute of North America; September 1982, pp.358–85.

Kalman, Harold. *A History of Canadian Architecture, Vol. 2.* Toronto: Oxford University Press, 1994.

Kaplan, Wendy (ed.). *Charles Rennie Mackintosh.* Glasgow: Glasgow Museums / Abbeville Press, 1996.

Killam, Sherry. "Coast to Coast". *Western Living.* Vancouver: June 1995; cover and pp. 29–34.

Lange, Bente. *The Colours of Copenhagen.* Copenhagen: The Royal Danish Academy of Fine Arts School of Architecture Publishers, 1997.

Lange, Bente. *The Colours of Rome.* Copenhagen: The Danish Architectural Press, 1995.

Lemon, Robert. "Our Estergreen: Remembering Robert Ledingham" *Western Living.* Vancouver, 13 July 2015, pp. 52–58.

Lemon, Robert. "Losses and Legacies: Vancouver's Burrard Street." *Conference Proceedings: Vision and Reality.* Stockholm: Fifth International DOCOMOMO Conference, 1998. pp. 216–19.

Lemon Robert. "Modernism in Context: learning from buildings of the modern era that fit in historic settings by being compatible, distinguishable and a product of their time." York: MA in Conservation Studies thesis, 1998.

Lemon, Robert. "Lives Lived: Mary Jean Johnson." Toronto: *Globe and Mail,* 5 April 2007.

Lyonnet, Jean Pierre (ed). *Robert Mallet Stevens, Architecte.* Paris: Éditions 15 Square de Vergennes, nd.

Magagnato, Licisco. *Carlo Scarpa a Castelvecchio.* Milano: Edizioni di Communità, 1982.

Morrissey, Jake. *The Genius in the Design.* New York: Harper Perennial, 2005.

Munro, Alice. "The Turkey Season." *The New Yorker.* 29 December 1980 issue. www.newyorker.com/magazine/1980/12/29/the-turkey-season

"New Perspectives on Heritage Conservation." Conference Brochure. Vancouver: Simon Fraser University, February, 1994.

Newman, John and Nicholas Pevsner. *The Buildings of England: Dorset.* New Haven: Yale University Press, 1972.

Palladio, Andrea. *Four Books of Architecture.* New York: Dover Publications, 1965; replication of original by Isaac Ware, 1738.

Pearson, Clifford A. "Island House and Tower House, Ontario." *Architectural Record,* April 2002, pp. 124–27.

Prat, Natalie. *Jean Prouvé.* Paris: Galerie Jousse Seguin / Galeric Enrico Navarra, 1998.

"Preserving 20th Century Curtain Walls" Conference Brochure. Vancouver: Simon Fraser University, September, 1997.

Prince, Rose. "Elizabeth The First". *Independent on Sunday*. 5 October 1997, pp. 7–12.

Saxon, Wolfgang. "Martin E. Weaver, Historical Preservationist, is Dead at 66." *The New York Times*, 31 July 2004.

Shaw, Catherine Elliot. *Fugitive Light: Clark McDougall's Destination Places*. London, Ontario: McIntosh Gallery, 2011.

"Seismic Retrofit of Heritage Buildings" Conference Brochure. Vancouver: Simon Fraser University, September, 1997

St. Thomas and its Men of Affairs. Richard Cochrill Limited, St. Thomas, 1976; reissue of original publication of 1914.

Stamp, Gavin, and André Goulancourt. *The English House 1860–1914: The Flowering of English Domestic Architecture*. Chicago: The University of Chicago Press, 1986.

Sykes, Meridith. "Parisian Architecture." Unpublished guide with maps of each of 20 arrondissements with typed lists of buildings.

Thau, Carsten og Kjeld Vindum. *Arne Jacobsen*. København: Arkitektens Forlag, 1998.

The Vancouver Foundation. "Historical True Colours for Western Canada." Vancouver and Aldergrove, BC: Vancouver Heritage Foundation and Benjamin Moore, colour sample brochure, nd.

Volloy, Dominique. *La Maison de Verre*. London: Thames and Hudson, 2007.

Venturi, Robert. *Complexity and Contradiction in Architecture*. New York: The Museum of Modern Art, 1977; second edition.

Weaver, Lawrence. *Houses and Gardens by E. L. Lutyens*. Woodbridge: Antique Collectors' Club, 1981; reprint of original Country Life book, 1913.

(✦)

INDEX

Note: Page numbers in italics refer to photos.

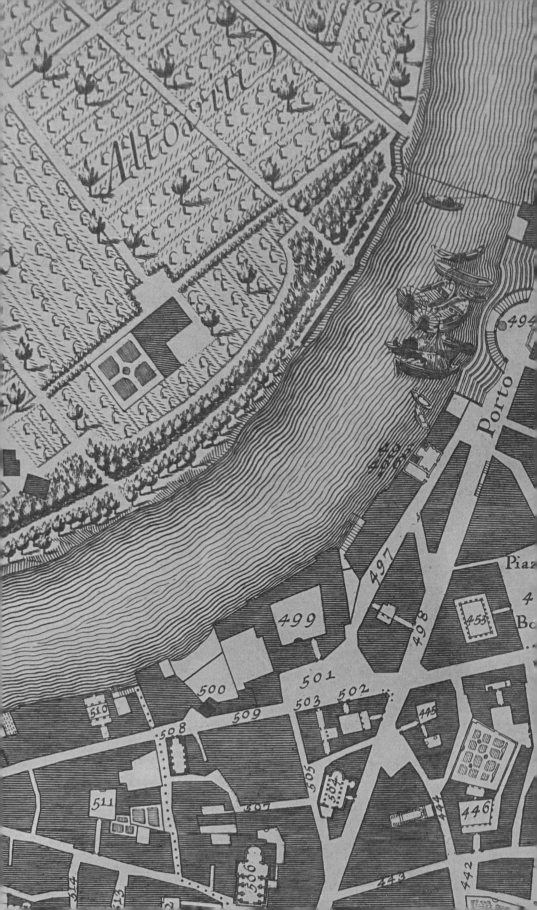